THE IMMATURE NATURALIST

MY DELICIOUS SALAD DAYS

by

S. C. SARDESAI

CLEVER FOX PUBLISHING
Chennai, India

Published by CLEVER FOX PUBLISHING 2024
Copyright © S. C. Sardesai 2024

All Rights Reserved.
ISBN: 978-93-56486-09-6

This book has been published with all reasonable efforts taken to make the material error-free after the consent of the author. No part of this book shall be used, reproduced in any manner whatsoever without written permission from the author, except in the case of brief quotations embodied in critical articles and reviews.

The Author of this book is solely responsible and liable for its content including but not limited to the views, representations, descriptions, statements, information, opinions and references ["Content"]. The Content of this book shall not constitute or be construed or deemed to reflect the opinion or expression of the Publisher or Editor. Neither the Publisher nor Editor endorse or approve the Content of this book or guarantee the reliability, accuracy or completeness of the Content published herein and do not make any representations or warranties of any kind, express or implied, including but not limited to the implied warranties of merchantability, fitness for a particular purpose. The Publisher and Editor shall not be liable whatsoever for any errors, omissions, whether such errors or omissions result from negligence, accident, or any other cause or claims for loss or damages of any kind, including without limitation, indirect or consequential loss or damage arising out of use, inability to use, or about the reliability, accuracy or sufficiency of the information contained in this book.

Dedicated to my parents—Jayashree and Sharad Shevade—without whom neither I nor the book would have come into being! And also to my husband, Shekhar—a partner in the truest sense!

CONTENTS

Preface .... *vi*

1. New Beginnings 1
2. Education—Informal and Otherwise 13
3. New place, New Experiences! 33
4. Friends—Human and Otherwise 51
5. Fascinating Flora 61
6. Daring Dalliances 79
7. Arboreal Amours 95
8. Random Reminiscences 105
9. Family Festivities 118
10. Expanding Horizons 136
11. Migrating Northward 156
12. Continuum 170

Postface *181*

PREFACE

*T*his effort has been a long time coming. In fact, I was downright apprehensive about the whole thing! But there was a ceaseless fluttering and whispering like a trapped creature under the surface of my creativity (if I may call it that), which I wanted to set free, and voila, this book was the result! If nothing else comes out of it, I will have at least improved my typing skills! Consider the book a memoir—memories of my nonhuman friends and acquaintances. These friends have been of the legged or legless categories; they have been feathered, furry or with nothing but a bald, smooth exterior! Hence the title.

If this narrative entertains some individuals while encouraging them to appreciate the highly complicated and interwoven fabric of life and if it makes them value the lives of our co-earthlings, I will consider it a success! I have expressly left out the more serious occasions which, sadly, all rescuers come across, as this rambling account is meant to leave the reader feeling refreshed and not depressed! This is a sincere hope.

I also DO NOT profess to be a professional zoologist or botanist. For the sake of the readers, I have done my best to do some research and provide as much accuracy as possible for me. But please do not take this to be a textbook of nature! It is just an effort to share the moments of our day-to-day lives with people who can relate to them and, hopefully, get some vicarious pleasure from perusing them.

So, I present to you some glimpses of the amazing and enriching encounters I had as a child.

P.S. Please pardon any small liberties I may have taken with the language or the order of events. Memory is a strange thing!

CHAPTER 1
NEW BEGINNINGS

*F*rankly, I don't think it BEGAN, per se. It feels like I was just born with a fascination for all the other creatures we homo sapiens share our one and only Blue Planet with. Most of my memories have some pet or the other enmeshed in the wispy threads of time. This preoccupation with Mama Nature and her varied creations has only increased by leaps and bounds as the years went by.

One of the earliest recollections I have is of me sitting on a rug in a school's nursery filled with toys, crayons and drawing sheets along with scores of bawling kids yelling for their moms! The walls were festooned with colourful and educational posters (this bit I realised in retrospect, of course, I was pretty much illiterate at that age). I remember clearly three motherly ladies valiantly trying to soothe all of us youngsters who had been heartlessly abandoned by their parents on that catastrophic day—THE FIRST DAY OF PRESCHOOL! Strangely enough, I don't think I was very upset; I was just awed by my surroundings. The posters were most fascinating: they had a C for cat, an E for elephant, an L for a lion with an unnaturally bushy mane, a P for a beautiful peacock with his tail spread out in full glory and last, but not the least, a T for a majestic tiger sprawled out in a verdant forest! Why do I remember that—don't ask! Then, there are the memories of the fables which were acted out by our long-suffering and sweet-natured teachers, which involved cunning jackals who escaped the fearsome king of the jungle, absolutely brilliant crows with a fantastic knowledge of physics who displaced water with stones and the silly fox who painted the town and himself blue! There were also clever monkeys, foolish crocodiles, brave mice and benevolent lions. Ever wondered how Indian folk tales are full of animals, and yet, once we reach adulthood, we seem to lose all that affinity towards them?

Our school day involved copiously colouring vivid birds, colourful fruit, disproportionate animals and consistently triangular mountains with the inevitable rising sun struggling to make its appearance! There were also times when all of us kids belted out various nursery rhymes discordantly; one had a poor puss which was thrown into a well by a mean boy, and yet another one had a guileless spider who was scared witless by a girl, all because it tried to share some of her food! As you can see, animal involvement is very much in evidence!

Fresh air was also an integral part of the curriculum, and we were regularly taken out to the playground for some fun and frolic. In other words, an insidious method by which our teachers could get us to do some unstructured exercise and also a way for getting kids to eat their snacks without making a total mess of the classroom! The school grounds were surrounded by old mango and *gulmohar* trees (Royal Poinciana), which had a whole bunch of feathered inhabitants—sparrows, pigeons, doves, babblers, bulbuls, etc. The white splatters on the slides and swings bore witness to their presence! If you were lucky enough to have an enthusiastic partner on the see-saw who enabled you to have a bouncing session on it, you felt as if you, too, could reach the leafy branches and join the feathered community for a quick chin-wag.

The main entrance to the school had a little concrete bridge over a man-made pond, which had fish darting in and out of delicate hydrilla plants which grew abundantly in it. All along the pond walls, tiny snails glided slowly over the algae grazing with seemingly insatiable hunger. An occasional dragonfly would dart by, distracting me from the frantic calls of the teacher, entreating us to get back into the classroom. From the classroom windows, you could see chattering palm squirrels dashing around madly, picking up any goodies which might have fallen from our tiffins. They would sit on their hind quarters, hold the food in their tiny yet perfectly formed paws and nibble delicately, their tails over their backs in a beautiful 'S' shape, which was the envy of all us kids who could barely draw a 'C'!

Going home was also a great adventure. All of us kids lived in a colony some distance away. This was the Northern township, set up exclusively for the employees of the Gujarat Refinery plant in Vadodara, of which my father was one. Our only mode of school transport was a dilapidated jeep in which we all piled in—literally (the stereotypical yellow school buses were not around in those days)! When, by some fluke, every student was present, and there was a dearth of space, I got the chance to sit at the very edge of the jeep on its half rear door, held in place by luck and Dilipbhai the helper, while the jeep trundled towards home sweet home.

Everyone would be lustily recalling the adventures of 'Jack and Jill' and 'Humpty Dumpty' while I desperately tried to listen to the sweet cooing calls of *koels* (a species of cuckoo in India) in the mango trees and the hooting of langurs feeding in the nearby farms over all the ruckus! Soon, we would arrive at my stop, where my mom would receive me. She would hold my hand, and we would begin the walk down the short, leaf-littered road leading home. All the time, I would be wondering exactly where I could grub about in the garden with my elder sister; she would guide me with all the worldliness of a seven-year-old kid. But inevitably, we would meet some 'aunties' on the way and, as good manners required, my mom would stop and exchange pleasantries, leaving me free to go and observe the big black ants marching determinedly in the dirt alongside the road. They were closely watched by colourful *Calotes versicolour* or oriental garden lizards, who would be perched in the hedge, bobbing their heads and flashing their crests to warn off others who had designs on their territory.

I have always found these creatures fascinatingly attractive—the way they change their colour from a brilliant orange to a dull green in a couple of seconds never ceases to amaze me! The beautiful black collar around the throat of the males makes them look like weird pet dogs. The females are not as flashy in appearance, but they do have a lovely crest and a dappled appearance with brownish markings. They would keep one eye on the line of ants and the other on me, cocking their head to one side, wondering if I was a threat or not. Suddenly, one would lean forward, flick its long sticky tongue out and then there was one less ant in the ranks! Fantastically efficient hunters but extremely territorial! They would fight tooth and claw over favourite perches until one of them finally conceded defeat and dashed off with his long tail stretched out behind him, frantically waving from side to side! I didn't realise it then, but all this was grist to the mill of my love affair with the animal world!

Life was very peaceful and yet never boring in the quiet little township we lived in. Everyone knew everybody else. There were plenty of open spaces to explore. For the more adventurous souls, the nearby fields beckoned temptingly. Not being faint-hearted (or, in other words, we simply didn't know any better!), a bunch of us decided to explore a nearby wooded area. I can still hear the wind swishing through the branches of the trees and the crunching of the dried leaves underfoot. The smell of the rampantly flourishing wild flowers was heavenly. No grownups were to be seen, and we could poke around in mysterious bushes and scramble up trees to our heart's content. All was right with the world! Then my big sis Shubhangi, or 'tai' (which means 'elder sister') as I called her, who has always been inclined towards botany, spotted a lovely climbing plant whose delicate green leaves were covered with soft, glossy hair. There were also bunches of beans likewise covered with tempting brown fuzz. She just couldn't resist touching them. They were indeed soft, but wait, they felt a little itchy! "Oh well, these things happen," we said while she dusted off her hand, and we decided to go on. But the itching wouldn't stop! It became worse by the second, and soon she was scratching away madly, like a dog with fleas, getting increasingly upset!

Luckily, before things became too bad, a farmer came to the rescue, and we realised we had stumbled upon a patch of *Mucuna Pruriens* or the *Velvet Bean* plant as it is commonly known, which causes extreme itchiness upon contact with any of the young leaves or seed pods. The home remedy for this involved rubbing the affected area with a cow dung patty (fortunately, an item which was easily available) which resulted in an extremely subdued and smelly sibling! The rest of us giggled all the way home, keeping a safe distance from the aromatic adventurer. But all said and done, the process was effective in ridding her of the itches! After this incident, we gave a wide berth to all plants tempting fur on them. This cautious attitude lasted for a few days but, as is wont with children, bad memories were soon forgotten, and we were ready and raring to go on with our intrepid explorations!

This time, we decided we needed to conquer a latticed red brick wall. It wasn't too high, and then there were many footholds—easy-peasy! So, the conquering heroines went full steam ahead and got up on the wall. Seniors went first, of course, and juniors followed in their footholds. From my small three-year-old viewpoint, the wall rose like a huge mountain, and I was Tensing Norgay to my sisters' Edmund Hillary. Suddenly, as is wont in the mountains, there was an 'avalanche' in the form of a loose brick, which got dislodged and came straight down onto my upturned face. The next thing I knew was that I was on the ground, and blood was pouring down my face. There was panic in the ranks as they all assumed that I was about to expire—and worse—they would all be blamed for my premature demise! Fortunately for all concerned parties, the incident only resulted in a throbbing headache and some missing hair from my eyebrow. I have a permanent scar to remind me of my foolish attempts to climb before I could run properly!

Around this time, we acquired our first dog.

My grandparents lived in the nearby Vadodara city and, on one occasion, while on the way to visit them, we came across a beautiful month-old puppy. He was a local breed with the characteristic rust-brown colour, floppy ears and melting eyes. We kids fell for him hook, line and sinker and wanted to take him home. We pleaded and whined and cajoled, but Mom said there was no way she could take care of yet another baby! As it happens so very often with moms, kid strategies were successful, and we took him home. We named him Tommy, which was quite the popular name in those days for dogs. He became our younger brother, companion, friend and comrade in mischief. He was given a regular bath so that he would not pass on any infection. Because the weather was cold, my mom would take him out on the sunny veranda, where she would rub him down with a towel so that he wouldn't catch a cold. The neighbours would hang over the dividing hedge, watching with great curiosity. It seems they even told my mom it was odd that she was taking as much care of the dog as she did of us! He had milk and chapatis the same as us, and when he was adjudged to have grown up sufficiently, he was even allowed tea, much to our chagrin—we were still considered to be too young for any!

Tommy had a routine. He would hang around the house most of the day, but in the evening, he would go out into the neighbourhood on his social round. Once back home, he liked to curl up in his favourite chair and take a nap. And he was pretty possessive about it! I remember we had a guest one day, and this person went and sat in Tommy's chair. At that time, Tommy was out gallivanting. The grownups progressed through exchanging pleasantries to refreshments. There was a relaxed atmosphere as everyone sat just enjoying the peace and quiet.

After a while, Tommy sauntered in and headed straight to the guest. He stood in front of the man and stared at him with piercing brown eyes. Now, Tommy was a big dog, and it must have been quite discomfiting to have him glaring at you. My mom tried to be a good hostess and ignored the unvoiced demands of her canine son, but the guest was obviously getting increasingly nervous. So, finally, she very apologetically asked the man to shift to another chair. Tommy promptly jumped onto his chair, curled up with a huge sigh and fell fast asleep, leaving my parents to explain the situation shamefacedly!

Tommy was basically a regular Indian pariah dog with all their characteristic traits of handsomeness, proud bearing and fierce loyalty. He could be the friendliest dog around, running up to people wagging his tail nineteen to dozen, jumping up and laughing into their faces. However, when it came to his family, he was extremely protective. A great example of his unflinching dedication and love was the time when my youngest sister, Vinita, was born.

The hospital where this joyful event occurred must have been a good six to seven kilometres away from our colony but—no clue how—Tommy found out that mom was in the sterile, strange-smelling building. He managed to sneak past the vigilant eyes of the nurses, and got into the room where mom and my baby sister were and got under the bed. From this place, he refused to budge! People who tried to do so were greeted with a view of gleaming teeth under a curled-up lip and a low rumbling sound like approaching thunder! No one, but NO ONE, except Mum, was allowed to handle the baby. The room had another new mom and her baby, but their visitors weren't allowed to enter the room either! Finally, my mom had to get up and take him out of the hospital and into my dad's car to be transported back home! I have always had the greatest admiration and respect for indigenous breeds—they are tough and resilient; you couldn't ask for a more loyal friend! They are also highly intelligent and resourceful, as they need to be to survive in the big, bad world. They are generally a very active breed and need to be exercised regularly, but that means that the upshot of this is a trim and fit owner. Personally, I feel that is a fantastic tradeoff!

CHAPTER 2

EDUCATION—INFORMAL AND OTHERWISE

*I*n Nature, there is treasure all around. All you need to do is go out and observe. The smallest clump of grass you find will be teeming with life: leafhoppers jumping from blade to blade, ants scurrying around trying to get at the grass seeds, the little blue butterflies hovering over tiny flowers, and where there are insects, birds will follow—bee-eaters swooping down for a snack, sparrows in competition with the ants for the seeds and possibly weaver birds wanting raw material for their nests! This is part of the irreplaceable web of life. Humans can survive solely due to the efforts of these and other supposedly insignificant creatures. According to one research, if we wipe out all the insects in the world, our species will manage to survive for merely five more years! So, to me, any form of life is nothing less than a treasure that contributes to our very existence, be it a plant or a tiny ant.

When I was about six years old, my family shifted from the Northern township to the newly built Southern township. So, we had newer and greener pastures to explore. Our home was a bungalow with a small yard in the front and a kitchen garden at the rear. A simple wire fence and hedges separated the neighbours' gardens. The colony was set amidst farmland, so we had quite a variety of creatures popping in and out of our yard. I remember the one time we had a peacock chick wander into it—what excitement! We immediately had visions of a pet peacock strutting about on our lawn and us being the envy of every single kid in the colony! So, we gave chase without even considering the fact that we had no idea how to raise one! Luck and agility were on the chick's side; it ran swiftly towards the hedge and dashed across the fence while we stood staring after it, our grandiose dreams in tatters.

Then there was the time we had a big grasshopper sitting on the top of the kitchen door frame. It was a lovely green colour with long legs and longer antennae probing the air gently. I was just getting out of the kitchen after fetching my dinner plate and was standing under the door frame admiring it when, with absolutely no provocation, he flew and landed on my little pinkie and bit me! Well, I exaggerate; grasshoppers don't bite. But I was barely six years old, so some drama and exaggeration were to be expected! The pricking sensation I had was because of the spurs on its legs and its little claws, which actually wasn't very painful, but the sudden visual of a large grasshopper whirring with large translucent green wings spread out and landing on my hand had really scared me, and I burst out bawling, insisting that the grasshopper had bitten me! My parents tried—futilely, I might add—to reason with me but finally gave up, applied some lotion on my pinkie and adorned it with a nice butterfly bandage. For a very long time after this incident, I gave grasshoppers a wide berth.

Our house was not a huge one: it was a two-bedroomed bungalow with a kitchen, a hall and a nice veranda in the front. My parent's bedroom had a lovely window with a wide and deep sill overlooking the gate. It made a very nice window seat on which we would loll, reading Mandrake comics or Enid Blyton books and munching on snacks. A room with definitely a great view! Thus, besides serving as a lounging nook, the sill served as an observation station. We could observe all the comings and goings in our lane and report back to mom. I even did my homework on the sill, supervised by my mom while she lay down for a bit of rest on the bed. As you can see, the window seat was rather popular with us all.

Our colony had a canal which ran through it, acting as a drain for the excess water from a neighbouring village pond. Even so, after especially heavy rains, it couldn't contain the massive volume of water being forced through it and so it spilt over, generously spreading its aquatic largesse all around. Sometimes, it would overflow so much that you could find fish in puddles quite a distance away. We would get some of these fish and house them in a pickle jar aquarium placed right in the centre of the aforementioned window sill. These fish were silvery, and the sunlight glinted off them as they darted about in the bottle. They had black streaks, and so we called them Zebra fish—a very apt name, we thought. Turns out, we were right! They were indeed Zebra fish. We didn't have any pet shops around in those days, and we fed them with little dough balls, which they ate quite happily, but it tended to make the water murky, and so, it had to be changed daily. Ultimately, the enthusiasm for observing fish lost out to the great effort it required to maintain the aquarium, and the fish would go back into the canal!

During the rainy season, we had a wide variety of non-human visitors. There were snails who crawled their way up on the outer walls of our home, leaving a pattern of crisscrossing tell-tale trails behind them as evidence. There were two main kinds, one with a pointed conical shell and the other with a flat spiral shell. They moved with their tiny shells swaying from side to side like little molluscan belly dancers twirling their hips as they made slow progress towards some algae patch. The path leading to the front door was a veritable highway for slugs who crossed it sedately without a care for their own safety, leaving behind their signature silvery tracks. We had to be really on alert and watch where we were going in order to avoid squashing the poor things.

There were also the gloriously beautiful Red Velvet mites. They would scurry about on the new baby grass, looking like little velvety animated rubies. They were so soft to touch that I wished I could keep on touching them. At that time, I hadn't known that these gentle and delicate-looking creatures were actually good hunters of other small insects, else their allure might have considerably diminished in my eyes! They are arachnids—like spiders—only very much prettier. I tried keeping them in a box with some green grass, fondly imagining that they were vegetarians, but never had the heart to keep them for too long in case they died on me! Sadly, these creatures are no longer found very easily in that part of the country-over-development and pesticides being a major reason, I am sure! The oil from these creatures is used for treating paralysis in traditional Indian medicine. So, the poor things must have also been over-hunted. Anyhow, we were content to stand and observe them trying to burrow under clods of earth or scurry over green tussocks. Occasionally, when the temptation became too much, I would pick up one and stroke its soft body for a bit before letting it continue its frantic perambulations amongst the weeds.

Then, there were the millipedes. You could see them scurrying around, their tiny legs so close together that their movement created an illusion of a tiny wave rolling along their sides, their little antennae waving around in a friendly fashion. They were mainly of two types: a cylindrical brown variety of the order *Julida* and a flat-backed one from the order *Polydesmida*. The cylindrical ones were pretty, like miniature sausages with white rings around them. They seemed to be least bothered about any comings or goings and merrily crawled over paths and walls, but if you tried touching them, they would curl up into tight spirals. They would wait in this position for a few seconds, and when they thought the coast was clear, they would uncurl and meander off as if nothing had happened. If you managed to have them walk on your arm, they tickled like the brush of a soft feather. During mating time, one individual carried around the other one on its back and went about its business just as usual, as if it had forgotten all about the important matter of procreation! I remember we children called them double-deckers, as in the buses! The flat-backed ones have the look of a small centipede, which makes you feel a little nervous, but, in reality, they are pretty harmless. This variety was happier in cracks and under stones and was larger than their rounded cousins. There were times when you discovered them crawling out of the bathroom drains and onto the tiles, and then there was only one thing to be done—yell for mummy and make her get rid of them!

If you stepped outside the house after a downpour, you would find that the front path was invariably littered with earthworms trying to escape their waterlogged burrows. I have spent quite some time trying to save all of them from being squashed by uncaring traffic—vehicular and pedestrian—but sadly, could not save all of these industrious farmer's friends. After the leaves of the rain-washed plants stopped dripping, and after the sun dried out the world a bit, you could see the lovely handiwork, rather the 'tail-end' work of these wriggling, boneless marvels of Nature. Earthworms literally eat the soil, and it passes through their system where all the possible nutrients from decaying roots, leaves and other dead creatures are extracted, and the rest of the soil comes out from the rear end and is deposited in beautifully coiled and curved shapes like miniature clay pots. Each heap could have passed for some expensive work of modern art if it was just a bit larger in size!

The monsoon nights were filled with the whirring of insect wings attracted by the street and veranda lights. Occasionally, a winged termite or a winged black ant would fly into your face. These creatures had delicate wings which came off easily, and, in the morning, you could see hundreds of wings at the base of the veranda light, which was left on in case some errant member of the serpent family decided to come up the steps. In the darkness, you could also hear a cacophony of wheezes, croaks and grunts as the bull frogs tried to attract mates. If you walked along the road, you could see the torchlight being reflected from enormous eyes popping out of each and every puddle. There were skipper frogs, swimming off swiftly with just a lazy kick of their legs; there was the common Indian toad who stared into space while its throat seemed to swell up magically, and a loud croak would emanate seemingly effortlessly from its depths. Then there was the huge Indian bullfrog or *Rana Tigrina*, with its beautifully pointed face, gold-edged eyes and a lovely camouflage pattern of leaf green with darker markings, which could have been the envy of any top designer! This pattern meant that you couldn't see them in between all the plants in the ponds. Only when they got startled and plunged into the depths would you know that there had been a frog there! They were always in competition with the toads regarding the volume of sound produced from greatly distended vocal sacs which made them look as if they had miniature inflated balloons stuck under their chins.

These besotted amphibian love songs resulted in masses of round, soaked-sago-like eggs in the deeper pools, which ultimately turned into scores of wriggling, black tadpoles. To supply them with company were writhing mosquito larvae which hung upside down on the surface of the pools. You just had to lean over a puddle and all of them would hastily wriggle to the bottom while the tadpoles would try to conceal themselves under rotting leaves and algae-covered pebbles. I would follow the progress of the inhabitants of a particular puddle with great interest. In a couple of months, most tadpoles had their front legs and looked like alien creatures from a far-off planet! A couple of weeks more, and they turned into tiny frogs with very long tails. By the end of three months, the puddle would be quite empty, and there would be the cutest, perfect, minuscule frogs hopping around its edge, trying to garner the courage to go out into the big, bad world and earn their insects.

The monsoons were an amazing time, bringing out the awesome and staggering wonder of nature in the form of the lashing rain, ringing thunder and jagged lightning across the wild sky! At night, you could lie all snuggled up in your bed and be lulled to sleep by the orchestra outside, which consisted of frogs croaking out their hearts in all sorts of pitches, crickets zinging away to glory, the occasional buzzing of a mosquito which managed to get into the mosquito net and in the background was the soft pitter patter of raindrops as if the environment was promising to let us have new puddles to explore the next

day. The rainy season brought new life into the world and taught us kids amazing lessons, the levels of which no regular school can ever aspire to attain. Mother Nature—the best teacher ever!

Sadly enough, there wasn't any way that Mama Nature could teach me to calculate the time in which two trains travelling in opposite directions would meet if train A was moving at X speed and train B was moving at Y speed (but shouldn't we have been more worried about the imminent collision, though?), nor could she teach me how to make water in laboratories (it was supposed to come from clouds, for heaven's sake!). And so—alas, alack—I had to attend a regular school!

Jokes aside, my school was not a bad place at all. I had a lot of fun AND I learned a lot during my time there. We had great teachers who had the patience of angels. The responsibility of running the school lay on the white-clad shoulders of our school principal, Father T. He was a strict man who allowed no running in the corridors, and we were all terrified of a thin, flexible, highly polished stick which he swung around nonchalantly on his school rounds. But behind all this mock toughness, he had a soft heart, and we could wheedle him into allowing us to do a lot of things which other school principals would have considered sacrilegious in those days. I remember he allowed me to keep tadpoles in his office as part of an experiment I had suggested. And when the poor things passed away because I didn't know better and caused a terrible stench, he did not reprimand me even once! In the third grade, he allowed me to organise a dance all on my own with a few of my friends and didn't say a word when I botched it up somewhat due to stage fright! It might have been many years ago, but he was definitely a forward-thinking principal who allowed us to try out things. Learning from one's own mistakes is a permanent lesson, indeed.

We were a small community; most teachers lived in the colony and knew our parents socially. You really had to watch out if you went shopping along with your parents in the local stores! You were bound to meet at least one teacher, and then you had it! All your school shenanigans were discussed as if you were invisible! There was absolutely no need for any parent-teacher evenings. In fact, I remember going and collecting report cards all on my own. If the teacher needed to say something specifically to the parents, they would just chat over the garden hedge while passing by or give a call on the local township phone.

All said and done, we had really good teachers. I remember Miss E with the greatest fondness. It is to her that I owe my love for science, especially biology. This love was further nurtured by Mrs. M. We also had a PE teacher, an ex-army man who taught us old English songs as a break from the traditional strenuous exercises and marching, and an excellent math teacher Mrs. P, without whose help I never would have cleared my board exam! I remember she coached me in the subject at her home totally free of charge and in fact, fed me delicious lunches when I was there. Her semolina-gram flour *ladoos* were absolutely divine. Try as I might, I haven't been able to find that exquisiteness anywhere! Incidentally, she was good friends with my mom, and so we really had to be on our toes; school escapades had a way of reaching my mom's ears without ever leaving home!

We had a Hindi teacher who did lovely *shayari*—a form of Hindi/Urdu poetry—and our head teacher, Mrs. Pr, to whom I owe my clear Hindi enunciation. Our art teacher, Mr. H, looked exactly like a stereotypical artist—longish hair, a long kurta, a typical sling bag on the shoulder and a slow saunter. He was very good at artwork and also loved acting. In those days, we were one of the few families with a tape recorder—yes, that sound sound—replicating machine with the two spools and a slowly winding tape—quite an ancient relic nowadays! So, my father offered to help with the sound effects of one of the school productions. I vividly remember how we did the recording for a storm scene at home: we were all told to shut up and hold our breaths; Dad would count down from three and press the record button, and then we would frenziedly begin our assigned tasks. I was to roll a heavy stone pestle from one end of the room to the other to create the sound of thunder; my mom was to pour water onto a sieve held by Vinita (my younger sister) so that it dripped down into a tub below and sounded exactly like the pitter-patter of rain while Shubhangi tai (my elder sister) shook an x-ray enthusiastically to create the sound effect for lightning! It was all going according to plan, but our dog, who thought he, too, should contribute to the family effort, decided that what the whole thing needed was a couple of woofs! That was the end of that session! The whole process had to be repeated with the canine safely locked away in the farthest room. I must say, though, the sound effects were remarkably realistic, and Mr. H was really pleased.

My English teacher—Mrs. S—could breathe life into the dead classics! She brought alive the romance in *Pride and Prejudice* and squashed all the sniggering of abashed teenagers. Very pragmatically, she helped us understand that love between the opposite sexes was a natural thing.

All my teachers were very accommodating about my passion for animals. There was an incident in school where a small injured bat was being harassed by some students. I plunged into the midst of the group and got hold of the petrified creature. In those days, I had no idea that such an innocent-looking creature was the carrier of the deadly rabies virus. As the saying goes, fools rush in where angels fear to tread! Thankfully, luck also favours the fool, and I did not come to any harm because of the poor thing. Anyway, that knowledge wouldn't have changed my decision to help the bat! This was the first time I had seen a specimen up close. It looked exactly like a cute mouse with leathery wings (which, of course, it isn't—it is actually related to lemurs and primates!) There wasn't much I could do as there were no vets for miles around. However, with the help of the erstwhile Dilipbhai, our staff helper, we dug into the depths of the staff room, and one of the bemused teachers, without much ado, very kindly emptied a shoebox. We used this as a kind of make-shift bed for the bat and placed him in a safe area on the roof, hoping its mates would help it out at night. We found it gone the next day, so hopefully, it recovered from whatever trauma it had undergone and flew off. I missed the better part of a class in the whole operation, but I did not get a word of admonishment! Not many teachers I know of would allow this kind of behaviour, but it is good souls like them that helped mould me into someone who cares about other living things.

Our school also organised quite a few trips in order to broaden horizons, as any good school does; there were, of course, the customary yearly class picnics to nearby picturesque spots, but besides this, out-of-station overnight trips were also organised by the school authorities. One such trip was a tour of the magnificent desert state of Rajasthan. Though more than sixty percent of Rajasthan is a desert, it is one of the most vibrant and colourful states. In stark contrast to the desert, the ethnic clothes of the Rajputs (as the local people are known) are very brightly coloured, often with tassels and embroidery. Women wear long skirts which swish elegantly as they walk, topped with beautiful waist-length blouses which are draped by a long length of cloth called the *odhni*. Men traditionally wear a typical long white top called the *angarakha* and a white pyjama or *dhoti*. The whole ensemble is topped by a brightly coloured turban on the head. Both men and women wear traditional footwear called *mojadis*. These are long slip-on shoes made from leather with a curling, pointy front. They are generally embroidered in bright colours with a bit of golden thread, adding to the vibrancy. Both men and women favour jewellery which is generally made from gold or silver, encrusted with stones. And it isn't just the attire which is colourful!

Rajasthan has a rich history full of courageous kings and brave queens who fought fiercely against invaders to protect their people. As you can imagine, this state has many beautiful forts and palaces, each telling its own story. Elephants, horses and camels were commonly used during battles, so they occupy an important place culturally. In fact, many domestic animals here have also been beautifully decked out with colourful saddles and elaborate ornaments through the ages. Especially the camels, elephants and horses. The city of Bikaner hosts the yearly Camel festival, which pays homage to the trusty 'ship of the desert.' Our teachers wanted to bring this rich history alive for us students, so the school tour was planned.

This trip was meant to be for the senior classes. But a few exceptions were made; I was in the third grade at that time, but one of my classmates whom we shall call 'U' and I were allowed to join the trip as Shubhangi tai was going. Although not even a student of the school, Cousin Vivek was also allowed to come along as an exception to the rule—the advantages of having a closely-knit parent and teacher community! The whole tour was an extremely exciting prospect for me, primarily because it was my first long trip without my parents and secondly because the entire trip was to be done by rail! The school had booked an entire coach for the students and accompanying teachers. This coach was to be our 'home' for the duration of the tour. When the routes changed, we were simply to be offloaded from one train and shunted on to the appropriate one; I can still remember waiting for ages in some back-of-beyond railway yard for the juddering 'thump,' which meant we had joined a new train. While we waited for this earth-shaking event (pun intended), we could observe the working of the Indian Railways yards—engines being cleaned, other coaches being washed, water tanks being topped up from tall pipes with gushing hoses swishing to and fro from the force of the water like angry, writhing anacondas—definitely educational experiences!

It was a two-tier coach, each compartment having four berths, two on each wall. All of us were assigned specific bunks. Shubhangi tai was given the lower bunk on one side while, due to his last-minute addition, the berth above her was to be shared by Vivek and me. Both of us being third graders and quite small, we fit quite comfortably on the narrow berth. I have always been quite a still and light sleeper, whereas Vivek would turn and toss. So, to prevent any fall, I was to sleep on the outer edge, which was fine with me. Despite this adjustment, there was still a dearth of space, so my classmate U was given the space on the floor between the two lower berths. A cook was part of the retinue, so home-cooked or rather 'coach-cooked' meals could be served. One end of the coach was converted to a makeshift kitchen containing massive vessels, some basic rations and a stove. Each time the train halted at a major station, fresh veggies were bought. However, we had a stock of potatoes and onions in case nothing else was available. The food tasted great, as it always does on picnics.

All went as per plan: we would chug along sedately till we reached a particular city and there we would be parked in a railway yard for a couple of days. Local transportation took us to the historical spots to do our sight-seeing. And what sights! Simply marvellous! Rajasthani architecture involves intricate carvings depicting people, animals and plants inside as well as outside the temples and other buildings. The structures themselves are made from sandstone or marble. A lot of the marble work has beautiful in-laid patterns made using stones, glass or mirrors, giving a very opulent ambience to the buildings. We were fortunate enough to see many of the palaces and forts in Chittorgarh, Udaipur and Jaipur—some of the important cities in the state. Most forts are situated atop steep hills, and quite a few tourists opted for an elephant back ride to reach them, unlike us poor students who trudged up all the way, casting envious glances at them—persevering pachyderms plying people!

After a long and tiring day of touring, a quick wash in a minuscule train toilet, some simple hot dinner and bedtime on a hard wooden berth seemed sheer luxury! All of us would be so tuckered out that we would fall asleep almost before the lights were switched off—the deep sleep of a truly tired body. No one got up until we were shaken awake by our teachers in the morning. One night, however, all of us were startled into wakefulness by the sound of a loud thud in our compartment and a painful scream followed by loud sobs! A teacher hurriedly switched on a few lights to investigate to find U in her bedding, moaning away, while Vivek sat blinking drowsily almost on top of her!

The scene was self-explanatory: Vivek had been rolling in his sleep, as was his habit, and being totally exhausted, I was absolutely dead to the world and did not register it, but he had somehow managed to roll over me and fall off the berth! Poor U had cushioned his fall, but thankfully, she was more shaken than hurt. Vivek was absolutely unscathed. In fact, he climbed back into bed and fell fast asleep immediately. The next morning, when the concerned teachers asked after any possible aches and pains, he was a total blank! He had absolutely no recollection of the commotion he had caused during the night! For us, it was one of the hilarious highlights of the train journey, but U looked daggers at him for days after that!

CHAPTER 3

NEW PLACE, NEW EXPERIENCES!

Around grade three, my dad got promoted, and we shifted into a much bigger house. This house came with a lot of space in the front as well as at the back for a kitchen garden. We even had a small enclosed courtyard that connected the house to the 'servant's' quarters, as they were called—rather insensitively, I thought! Actually, the household help we had was more like family to us, and my parents took it upon themselves to improve their lot. (To date, we visit them in their beautiful two-storied house, and very often they drop us back in their brand-new car!) At the time we shifted into the new house, two members of a poor farming family—a widowed mother and her young son Rai—came to live with us. There were also hordes of relatives who came in turns and stayed with them until they found jobs and then shifted to their independent accommodations. We learnt a lot from them all as they had a good knowledge of how to live off the land. Our front garden bloomed as my parents toiled hard on it along with them. In fact, one year, we entered the competition for the best garden in the district and stood second! My mom couldn't be prouder!

There were beautiful roses of various colours grafted by my mother herself. A Cycas tree which was her pride and joy, was in the place of honour at the top of the garden and a beautifully manicured hedge grew all along the front edge of the garden. She even tried her hand at topiary, and we had a 'plant bird' of a totally unique species on our garden hedge for quite a long time, which vaguely resembled a peacock but was a variety undiscovered by the zoological world! The flower beds were artistically curved and edged with large white pebbles which glistened in the bright sunshine. To procure these, we made exciting trips to the nearby river and got them by the sackful. These pebbles had been beautifully rounded by the rolling waters, which caused the rocks to rub against each other till they were worn down to smooth cobbles. A few large and beautiful shells also added to the attractiveness of the flower beds. The cobblestones also decorated a beautiful rockery, providing the 'desert' look for mom's cacti collection. A bit incongruously, but most artistically, this rockery was surrounded by a fish-shaped moat made of concrete and created entirely in-house.

Obtaining all the raw materials for the flower bed edging was a wonderful adventure and a pleasure involving a riverside picnic. The spot we went to was about an hour away. The route took us out of our colony gates, through the outskirts of a village where the car would be chased vociferously by stray dogs guarding their territory, then past the huge refinery, which was my dad's workplace and onto a narrow and rather bumpy track. After some time, we would reach a mini colony set up by the refinery for the local staff, aptly called 'Headworks' (headworks are concerned with intakes from a waterway). Their duty was to manage the huge wells that supplied water to the refinery and the colony.

The river had a wide basin courtesy of massive flooding during the monsoons. At these times, the mild river turned into a raging sea, hurtling tons of water towards the Arabian Sea, the level of which came up to—and sometimes even went over—a bridge which had been constructed at the height of over twenty metres above the ground! Our dad took us to see the river in full spate one rainy season. It was an awesome visual but humbling as well to know that the gentle river could unleash such destructive power!

Fortunately, our excursions to this lovely riverside would occur during the springtime when the weather was pleasant, and the river was more of a meandering stream. We would park our car on one edge of the wide channel and make our way down to the river using pathways created by shepherds and cattle who used the river as their source of water. There were reports of leopards coming down to drink water from nearby woody areas—probably true in those days when deforestation wasn't so rampant! I always kept a sharp lookout for any sign of a big and bold cat that may wish to join our picnic, but fortunately, good sense prevailed on their part, and they never deigned to do so!

We would gingerly cross the wide bank which was covered with coarse sand and bits of broken shells shimmering in the heat. Chappals seemed to sink into the sand at the drop of a hat, so our feet were always bare. After reaching the river's edge, the first thing to be done was to cool off our hot feet in the softly eddying waters! It made a soothing, gurgling sound as it went over the pebbles, occasionally rolling them over and scaring the tiny fishes that hid underneath. There were the occasional boulders strewn across the river, which we used as stepping stones to explore further into the river. We would have a wonderful time splashing about in the water while observing the aquatic *Vallisneria* grass waving gently in the flow, the sedately moving snails inching over algae-coated rocks, the darting fish and the occasional shrimp, which were small and almost transparent.

Finally, we would go around collecting rounded cobbles, dump them in a jute sack, and then lug them across the gleaming white sand to be dumped in the car boot. But before our return trip, we would be invited for lunch at the Headworks colony by one of Dad's colleagues, Nair Uncle, as we called him. He was a dab hand at making fried fish, which I adored (in those days). And if we were in a real hurry, he would pack a good amount in a steel tin to be taken back home. The fish was fresh from the river and was finger-licking good! I still think of that gentleman fondly for all the kindness and consideration he showed us. And then, finally, we would be homeward bound!

Once we reached home, the stones would be scrubbed clean under the tap, dried and then used to edge all the flower beds. The rose garden had very artistic freeform edging while there were two ovals in the centre of our neat lawn, which were home to seasonal flowers like dahlias, chrysanthemums, the aptly called 'dog-flowers' or snapdragon and the dianthus, which added a delicate scent and glorious hue to the already colourful garden not to mention that it created another feeding station for innumerable insects. One edge of the garden had Ashoka trees, which housed quite a few kinds of birds, including sparrows, bulbuls, prinias and the occasional squirrel. A big casuarina tree at the beginning of the garden also served as a perch for bigger birds like crows, koels and babblers. A *thuja* shrub (belongs to the cypress family) next to it was pruned to an oval shape and was home to a tailor bird. It was amazing to see how beautifully the nest had been constructed; the elongated leaves were all tied up at the base with the help of long grass blades, and then the upper edges were sewn together to form a cup that was lined with soft grass and bits of cotton to form a comfortable bed for four glossy blue eggs which were dotted with tiny brown splotches. It was very well camouflaged because of the use of the live leaves. The leaves continued to thrive and remain lush; thus, the nest remained very well hidden while the fledglings grew, and no cat or fox could ever spot it.

At the far end of the formal garden, there was a bushy bougainvillaea and a frangipani plant whose sweet-smelling blooms invited the assiduous attentions of the hawk moths at night. A huge Rangoon creeper (*Madhumalti*) had draped itself over a decorative wall by the front veranda, and it was also a strong rival for the attentions of the hawk moths and butterflies; numerous huge rose-pink bunches of flowers cascaded down the wall looking like a pink waterfall, so there was always enough to go around for all the nectar sipping *lepidopteras*. It was a source of food for them and a hiding place for reptiles like geckos, garden lizards and skinks. Basically, it was survival of the fittest: if a butterfly was quick-witted and alert, it could have a tasty snack; a little carelessness, and it could end up as a snack for one of the lizards!

Our garden was separated from the neighbours' yard by a lantana hedge whose flowers were so profuse and colourful that anyone could easily get bedazzled. This riot of flowers was the local bar for a great variety of butterflies. There was the Common Sulphur, the dancing Jezebel, the royal Monarch and the beautiful little Pansy species, which always seemed to be in a hurry to go somewhere and would busily open and shut its wings, giving tantalising glimpses of the rich colours inside.

At the end of the garden at ninety degrees to the frangipani, was a row of jasmine trees which, when in full bloom, appeared to have miniature scented snowballs stuck on them. And in the corner of the garden, the beautiful Mater-designed rockery rose gently to create a contrast to the smooth lawn. The boulders and stones were courtesy of the aforementioned river bed. On it were strategically placed cacti and aloe vera, whose flowers were a favourite with the glistening purple sunbirds. A tap located next to the rockery seemed to drip ever so gently no matter what! This dripping tap was a boon to the fauna as well as the flora in the scorching summer heat. You could see all the birds swoop down, turn by turn, and hang onto the tap, gulping the drops of the precious elixir. And it wasn't just the birds.

As our house bordered farmland, we had quite a few visitors who slithered in to pay a visit—huge big cobras and nonvenomous rat snakes. They repaid us by keeping down the number of rats and mice who hid in the kitchen garden. One thirsty cobra found the tap so convenient that he decided to take up residence in the rockery which had a few crevices and holes. He could be seen on occasions curled up under the tap, raised hood and open mouth, waiting for the drops to fall into his throat and slake his thirst. My father believes in the adage of live and let live so we did not harm him; only we were very, VERY careful to take a torch with us if we had to venture out into the garden at night.

One day, around dusk—a very confusing time of the day because it isn't dark enough to warrant lights, yet the trees cast long shadows due to the setting sun—my mom and Shubhangi tai were standing on the veranda chatting with my dad who stood on the driveway a mere two steps down. They were chatting casually, enjoying the cool evening breeze which was laden with the fragrance of the surrounding flowers, when suddenly Shubhangi tai turned white as a sheet and started whimpering. Concerned, my parents asked her what was wrong, but she just whimpered and then pointed to the ground. My dad looked down just in time to see a cobra between his feet, all coiled and ready to strike. Being a man of common sense and quick action, he immediately jumped as high as he could! At the same time, the cobra struck and hit its head against the hard tar of the driveway. That in itself must have been disheartening for the snake, and

when my dad landed with a thump next to it, it just gave up and decided to retreat to its lair in the rockery.

I don't believe in the least bit that the cobra came out with the intention of biting anyone. Snakes take a long time to make venom which they need to kill their prey and feed themselves. So, generally, they would try to conserve it instead of wasting it on big and bulky mammals, which they cannot consume anyway. Probably, the snake had been heading home and suddenly found its way blocked by shuffling feet. Even that would not have been a problem, but all the whimpering and loud voices must have likely scared it into attacking (new studies show that snakes can hear a range of airborne sounds). Thankfully, it was all's well that ends well for us. Sadly, it did not end very well for the snake. A few weeks later, a couple of mongooses decided that the rockery would make an excellent nursery and had it vacated—whether by fair means or foul, we never found out.

Not satisfied with just a pond moat, my mom had the idea of creating a meandering stream emerging from the rockery, as if from a mountain and ending in a shallow pool a few feet further down. It looked really pretty as the water gently burbled down the channel but unfortunately, the stream would keep getting clogged with falling leaves from the surrounding shrubs and became rather a high-maintenance feature. So, reluctantly, my mom had it removed, and we lost a much-enjoyed paddling stream.

New place, New Experiences!

After we shifted into this particular house, we were offered a German Shepherd puppy. One of my dad's colleagues' pets had been blessed with a litter of thirteen puppies, and he desperately needed to home them. And so, Robinson Crusoe (we had just finished reading the book!) arrived home at the ripe old age of twenty-one days!

He was the cutest puppy ever, whose tummy was bigger than his legs so that if he tried to trot, his belly would get in the way, and he would fall flat on his face! He had the most soulful melting eyes, and his ears were all floppy. As we had no idea about the species, we decided that he wasn't really an Alsatian—not that it mattered—but of course, as he grew, his ears perked up one at a time so that for some weeks he looked sort of lop-sided with one cocked up ear and one floppy ear.

Every evening, we played a game of catch on the lawn with Robby, as he came to be known. He was so cute that all our friends came to give him a cuddle and received wet, frenzied licks in return. But Shubhangi tai's best friend, who visited regularly, was petrified of him! The picture of a strapping fifteen-year-old girl running round and round my sister, panting and screaming, "Get him away from me!" at the top of her lungs with a tiny pup trying hard to keep up with her and tripping after every few steps, is permanently etched into my brain! We were convulsed with laughter at this ridiculously funny-looking spectacle, simply unable to go to her rescue. At the end of five minutes, there were breathless siblings, a very upset and exhausted teenager and a panting puppy who just couldn't understand what all the commotion was about—he just sat and grinned up at us because we were laughing and forgot all about his object of interest—much to her relief!

Of course, this friend soon fell for Robby's charms, as did most people who met him. He grew up to understand our language very well (as have all our dogs and cats) and was a docile and obedient chap. One evening, when we were taking Robby on his daily constitutional, another German shepherd being walked slunk up unnoticed behind him and bit him hard on his tail. Robby, who walked off leash, snarled and turned to retaliate, but my dad told him to stand down and instantly, despite no leash, he stopped and satisfied himself with growls and snarls! This obedience was not the result of any strict training but an inborn sense of obedience and respect. He was one of the most self-controlled dogs I have known.

When he was about ten years old, a tomcat literally walked into our lives and decided to stay on. Now, a dog as big as Robby, who had hardly seen a cat before except for chasing the odd one in the garden, could easily have killed 'Big Cat'—as we called the tom—but just because we told him not to attack, he let the tom come in and out of the house without ever chasing him. That is not to say

New place, New Experiences!

he was thrilled with the prospect of sharing his home and family with a feline, but he was a thorough gentleman! Later, a rambunctious little Doberman pup joined the family, and poor Robby bore it all with just an occasional raising of his expressive yellow eyebrows and by heaving deep, long-suffering sighs.

Robby had one weakness, though, which he simply couldn't overcome. And it was rather unexpected! Our kitchen had a small larder/storeroom attached to it. My mom used it to store big drums of grain, extra vessels, tea, biscuits—basically everything that was not required on a daily basis. Extra onions and potatoes were also stored in a mesh basket on a low stand. One fine day, Mummy saw the potatoes were in short supply, and so they were replenished. The next day, despite not having used any, the potatoes were missing again! Mom asked us if we had used up any for some weird playtime activity, but we hadn't. She checked with Rai if, perchance, he had taken any for cooking something, but he vehemently denied this. We girls were thrilled—a real live puzzle—'The Mystery of the Missing Potatoes'! This strange disappearance of potatoes continued for quite a few days; nothing else went missing, just potatoes! As Alice (in Wonderland, of course) said, "Curiouser and curiouser!" Our detecting skills were sadly lacking and produced no results—the potato thief remained at large!

One afternoon, when lunch was all done, and Mum was headed to her bedroom for a siesta, she suddenly remembered some chore and went to the kitchen where she caught the perpetrator in the act—it was Robby, sneaking out from the store with a nice crunchy, juicy potato in his mouth!1 Upon being caught, the poor boy's tail went down, and he hung his head all through my mom's reprimands. Mystery solved!

Now, we produced quite a few veggies in the kitchen garden, and that year, we had a big quantity of new potatoes. These needed to be aired before being put away. Mom warned Rai not to leave the potatoes at dog level in the store, but Rai, not having witnessed Robby's partiality towards spuds, just shot her a look of disbelief and completely ignored her instructions. He had never heard of a dog eating raw potatoes! Cows and goats, maybe, but dogs—no way! The fresh-smelling potatoes all laid out neatly were too much of a temptation for Robby, and he picked one and shot off, leaving Rai staring open-mouthed after him. After this, the storeroom door was kept firmly shut. But we never could resist the big, soulful Alsatian eyes, and he was allowed a potato or two on occasion as a treat. And potatoes weren't Robby's only passion. He simply adored papayas, mangoes, carrots and the likes; he had probably been a goat in his previous life!

German shepherds have delicate legs and are prone to breaks. When he was about eleven, Robbie stumbled on the doorstep and broke one of his front legs. Our vet said the chances of full recovery were slim as he was a senior-ish dog and not so strong. We were devastated and decided that we had to prove the vet wrong, but it was an uphill task.

First of all, Robbie hated being unable to go and relieve himself in the garden as usual; he struggled to go out to do his business despite our pleading and telling him it was perfectly okay to go in the room itself. Ultimately, when he could no longer hold it in and had to pee where he was sitting, he would be most embarrassed and would feel very guilty despite our assurances. My dad would have the morning duty of giving him a wipe with Dettol water and then with eucalyptus oil in the hope that the flies would be kept at bay, but no such luck!

One horrifying evening, as I was cleaning him, I noticed an open wound the size of a quarter under one of the hind legs. I could see something wriggling in it! I let out a yell and everyone dashed over, thinking the worst. We all thought Robby had got some horrible disease and immediately sent for the vet. After a look at the wound, he informed us that this was actually caused because poor Robby could no longer ward off the ever-present flies, and they had laid eggs on him. Those gross wriggling things in the gaping hole were maggots who were feeding on the flesh. Once in a while, they would stick their heads out for a breather before diving back into the blood!

I can't imagine how much my poor Robby must have been suffering, being gnawed at continuously and unable to do anything about it! The vet gave us some chloroform, a few drops of which we would put into the wound. After a couple of minutes, we would take a pair of tweezers and pull out the sleeping or dead maggots. It was one of the grossest things I have ever done! Unfortunately, despite our best efforts with the eucalyptus oil and the Dettol, Robby had a few more of these open sores over the next few days. So we all took turns to do this maggot fishing because even if a single maggot remained, the wound wouldn't be able to close up! Eventually, the holes closed, and Robby felt good enough to limp around.

But now came another problem; it was time for our annual vacation, and this time, we were going to the next state to visit Shubhangi, who was studying in a college there at the time. There was no way we could leave our beloved dog in this condition. Still, it was imperative to meet my sister, who was staying away from home for the first time and whom my parents desperately wanted to meet. My dad came up with a brilliant solution: we hired a van in which comfortable bedding was put down in the aisle for Robby. The rest of us (our family and my uncle's family) piled in, and off we all went for a fifteen-day trip! At rest stops and gas stations, people would gaze with bemusement at the sight of a bunch of kids laughing and chattering and a limping dog joining the conversation with woofs. In those days, dogs were generally used as guards and weren't considered part of the family.

All our pets have been fanatically crazy about my mom, probably because we kids were instrumental in bringing them home, but mom was the one who actually took care of their needs and was there for them the whole day while we went to our respective educational institutions. I would have happily given up studying in order to take care of them, but this suggestion would have been vehemently overruled! The long and short of it was that they all worshipped the ground she walked on. Robby was no exception. He refused to let her out of sight, even in his three-legged state.

At one point in our vacation, we visited a hill station. Among the must-see sightseeing spots was a viewpoint which had a fantastic location but had an extremely uneven and precarious approach. We had to park the van quite a distance away and then trudge laboriously along a rocky path to reach the viewpoint. My mom went ahead to take a gander, and before I could get down and shut the door, Robby hopped off and gave chase, teetering on his three legs. I was sure he would fall over the cliff and yelled for mummy. She came back up the path quickly, and the relief we saw on Robby's face was so palpably funny! I am sure he thought my mom was in some kind of danger, and he had to save her! From that day on, Robby recovered by leaps and bounds—pun intended!

The vet always maintained that he recovered from his fracture because we cared enough to take him with us on the vacation, which gave him a psychological boost. He was with us for two more precious years till he passed away because of other age-related problems.

CHAPTER 4

FRIENDS—HUMAN AND OTHERWISE

*A*s I mentioned earlier, we had shifted into a bigger bungalow when I was in grade three; this house was some distance away from the school. It took about fifteen to twenty minutes to walk back home at a brisk pace, but then, I wouldn't really know because we were never in a hurry! There were plenty of distractions en route to keep us occupied. So, it would take us anything from a half hour to three-quarters of an hour. Many were the times when Rai (our house help) would be dispatched on the bicycle to hunt us down and prod us into picking up speed, as my poor mum would be waiting hungrily to have lunch with us before taking a well-deserved siesta. My sister and her friend would start off from school at a slow pace, pausing every few feet to discuss some topic in depth, oblivious to the hot sun and to other students rushing home. Mrs. P, the Math teacher, who stayed in the same general direction, would clear her throat loudly as she swept past with her customary umbrella held up to protect her from the glaring heat. She would feel duty bound to pause and reproach the girls and get them to hurry up as their "mums were waiting." She would also feel obliged to stop by our gate and inform my mom about their location so that Rai could zero in on them!

Me, I prudently took a slightly roundabout route—one which just happened to pass by some interesting spots! Actually, there were quite a few of us who would trudge back home together. As each classmate's home neared, they would slowly and reluctantly leave the group like a leaf falling off a branch. There was a short cut through a low-lying plot of land which, strangely, occupied us for a loooong time! The rough and narrow path created by the tramping of numerous feet snaked through a dense overgrowth of Black honey shrubs and tangled grass dotted with wildflowers struggling to rise up towards the sun in some open spots. It was a small patch of untouched wild vegetation which was home to a host of flitting butterflies, frisky grasshoppers and tiny leafhoppers which scattered like confetti as our feet swished through the long grass. A variety of beetles scuttled frantically to get out of our way as we made our way clumsily through their territory. These, of course, attracted dashing lizards who eyed us coldly from their hiding places in the bushes where they bided their time, waiting for the right time to ambush their prey. There were also shy geckoes with beautiful golden eyes whose camouflage was so good as to be almost invisible, and graceful skinks who glistened in the sun as they scurried away and hid under fallen leaves. These have a snake-like look because of their short legs, sinuous movement and smooth, glistening scales. Because of this, many people consider them venomous, but in reality, the poor things are very innocuous lizards.

Our whole group would stop once in a while, scouring the shrubs for fruit. Occasionally, one of us would start a game of 'hide-behind-a-thicket-and-jump-out-unexpectedly' to startle others engrossed in munching the tiny ripe Black honey shrub berries. This invariably resulted in a lot of accusations and counter-accusations being flung about and a brief game of catch-the-culprit. Soon—egos satisfied—peace would reign, and everyone would return to the serious task of eating the berries. The small fruit had a mildly sweet taste, and the not-so-ripe ones were slightly tart, but that did not deter us! The main appeal was the thrill of plucking wild berries and eating them, just as any Famous Five member from the Enid Blyton series would have done. The berries would stain our lips and tongues an inky colour, and there was always a competition to see whose tongue was the darkest shade. We would all stick out our tongues, which were as blue as any giraffe's and then squint down our noses, trying to see who had won the round for that day. Unfortunately, the berries could also stain school uniforms, which was a point of contention with the moms. Fortunately for us, the stains, though tough, were not permanent—not on the tongues, nor on the clothes. During the rainy season, a puddle would collect at a particular spot right on the path, and this was a favourite spot for frogs to spawn. We would crouch down and observe the tadpoles for ages, oblivious to the time and pangs of hunger. Ultimately, one of the others who wasn't as crazy about critters would urge us onwards to our real destination—the canal.

This canal, which I have mentioned previously, began at a village pond some distance away from the colony. It ran through the colony and out into some fields beyond the colony, carrying any excess water away from the village so that it did not get flooded. This was the best time to observe a large variety of aquatic life—simply by sitting on the little cement ledges built on either side of the road, which spanned the canal, allowing the water to flow underneath it. Depending on whether it had rained heavily the night before or not, the water would be a swirling, muddy, raging mini river or a calmly flowing clear stream. On the sides of the canal, you could see tiny fish, their bodies writhing and fins flapping in an effort to maintain their position in the current. In the centre, you could see huge big catfish staying low, their long

barbels streaming behind them. They were a favourite with some of the village people hired as house help by township residents, and they would try to catch them for making fish curry. They were not an easy catch! I have seen the bloody footprints left on the road by one such hopeful where the fish got his heels with the spines they have behind their fins! The sight gave us kids a macabre thrill, and we would pore over the prints daily, imagining all sorts of gory scenarios till the rain finally washed them away.

Occasionally, you could see a turtle poking its head out of the flowing water to take a breath before disappearing amongst the weeds. Some of these turtles could be found quite far away from the canal during times of incessant rain. We had a rescued turtle in our courtyard for quite a few days till he decided he had had enough of a cloistered existence and simply dug his way out!

To get back to the canal, if you were lucky, you could spot a chequered keelback slithering out of the big pipes, which let the canal water flow under the road. I loved to watch these nonvenomous snakes in action! They are extremely graceful in the water, and the pattern on their back, which gives them their name, is really attractive. They would start by first tentatively poking their slim head out of the pipe, flicking their tongue testing the air for any danger. If we remained absolutely motionless, they would slowly slither out of the pipe to swim gracefully to the nearest boulder and hide under it. They would then wait there for some unsuspecting fish to pass by and snap! In a trice, the fish would be gone.

The whole canal had a load of insects hovering over and in it: dragonflies in fluorescent red, yellow and blue, swooping over the canal and the puddles, occasionally hovering over us as if wondering how on earth we fit into the landscape! Then, there were the iridescent damselflies flitting in between the dragonflies. You could be forgiven for thinking that the two were the same type of insects, with the damselflies being smaller and thinner members. But when they perched on the little twigs poking out of the water, you could see the most obvious difference—the wings of the dragonflies are held out away from the body whereas a damselfly folds its wings and holds them over its body.

Then, there were the omnipresent mosquitoes whining around you, and if you happened to stay still for a minute or so, they would zoom in for a quick snack! The surface of the water would be rippling lightly with long, thin Water striders using it exactly like a skating rink, gliding around with their long legs. There were whizzing Whirligig beetles which went round and round swiftly in circles. Considering their speed, it is quite amazing that they don't bump into each other! It made you feel quite dizzy just to look at them. There were also Water Boatmen who used their legs as oars. The flies would buzz around busily, stopping occasionally to taste a snack from an open tiffin box as someone tried to stuff it down their throat before reaching home in order to avoid a parental lecture about nutrition and the importance of eating at the right time. Any spillage was quickly attended to by big ants, which tramped up and down invisible ant-roads. The leafhoppers and butterflies skipped from bush to bush, with an occasional bumblebee busily coming in to inspect the flowers. The sparrows and crows would fly down occasionally and scold us for not sharing our snacks with them. The place was a hot spot for critters!

Generally, by this point, one of the mothers would spot us from their veranda and would holler for the kid to go home. Reluctantly, we would part, coming down to earth and guiltily comparing information about the home assignments due the next day. One set of friends would drift away while the rest of us would proceed leisurely to our next spot under some shady *gulmohar* trees. While we stood there chatting, the yellow blossoms and dried leaves would gently float down and create a carpet around our feet. There was also a bus stop nearby where one could observe the occasional company bus plying its passengers. Here, we would hang around till another mom spotted us.

So, it continued until, finally, I was the only one left. This did not deter me too much, though, for there was one more extremely interesting spot before I reached home. There was a cement pit about five feet deep and three feet wide next to the road just about five minutes away from home. This was made to gain access to a valve on a water pipe. This valve seemed to leak perpetually, so the pit was always filled with water. This spot was a veritable aquarium—there were big fat toads with knobby skins floating on the surface with legs spread out, looking like animated "X'es". A few bullfrogs who would disappear with a loud splash as you approached. There were wriggling mosquito larvae in various stages of development: stick-like younger ones who hung upside down on the surface to breathe and wriggled down to the bottom if you so much as cast your shadow on them; and then there were also the comma-shaped mosquito pupae who mostly hung around at the muddy bottom as if they had fallen out of an English essay. Again, there were the usual snails gliding through the green algae-covered sides, which were covered with tiny bubbles of oxygen. It looked as though someone had stuck tiny moonstones on green velvet all around the inside of the tank. Whirligig beetles and huge, big striders danced on the smooth and clear surface of the water.

I would peer into this mesmerising world for ages, hypnotised by the zipping beetles, which went round and round in circles and suddenly, the frantic ringing of a cycle bell would penetrate my trance as Rai sped towards me to take me home, where everyone was waiting hungrily!

CHAPTER 5

FASCINATING FLORA

Our colony—as is usually, and regrettably the case most times—was built on farmland. When the construction was done and roads made, almost all traces of the fields were wiped out. Most of the original trees were cut down, and *gulmohar*, neem, the beautiful Cassia fistula or golden rain tree with its gorgeous tumbling flowers like bunches of golden grapes and other big shady trees were planted alongside the roads. When they were in bloom, the sides of the road were a riot of colours, and the road itself looked as if petals had been strewn in the honour of approaching royalty. But here and there, wherever possible, someone with a sense of responsibility had left the original endemic trees alone. There were some mango trees with their thick, blackish-green leaves and the totally contrasting soft, reddish-purple new leaves. Sometimes, we would pluck these baby leaves, sprinkle them with salt, and then roll them up and chew them like seasoned 'paan' (betel leaf) eaters, complete with the champing sounds! Frankly, the leaves have a slightly bitter taste, but it made us kids feel very adventurous; we were living off the land!

Mango leaves are considered auspicious in India, and on any festival, you would see that the main entrance door of the homes would have a garland of these leaves with an occasional marigold strung up on top. Religiously, it is considered to ward off evil and also considered to be associated with some Gods. Scientifically, it is said to kill some types of bacteria and fungi. They are also used in some Ayurvedic medicines.

Then, there were some huge tamarind trees. One was just outside the school grounds. When the tree bore flowers and fruit, it was a favourite haunt of us kids. The ones on lower branches could be reached with a few athletic jumps. Wish our PE teacher had thought of hanging a few above the high jump poles—we would certainly have put in much more effort! The flowers were small, a pretty yellowish-white colour, and mildly sour when eaten. The fruit itself was actually a bean which was green when raw and turned a deep brown as it dried. Both versions could be eaten. The Indian tamarind is really sour, and our faces would pucker up till the cheeks almost met inside our mouth, but that was certainly not going to put off intrepid kids like us! Sometimes, the fruit would be just out of reach and took quite a bit of effort to obtain, and the fruits of our labour definitely tasted sweet! There was a trick to enhance the taste as well; sprinkling some salt and chilli powder made them quite lip-smacking. But we children never had the patience for all those niceties. In fact, the thought of washing them before eating never even entered our minds. Pluck, dust and pop into the mouth—that was the way to go!

In India, tamarind is used for a lot of cooking—from chutneys to certain curries. So invariably, each kitchen has some dried and salted tamarind as it can be preserved for a very long time in this way. In fact, a company has come out with a similar mix offered as refreshing sweets. A very refreshing summer drink is also made using tamarind. I would sneak some from the kitchen jar and hide them under my pillow—much to my mother's intense irritation as it spoilt the bedsheet and pillow case—and then proceed to suck on them while reading my collection of comics and adventure books. In my defence, they are a healthier snack than most other store-bought stuff. The tamarind seeds have quite a few medicinal benefits. We would collect a sizable number and roast them in a 'Chula,' an earthen stove made by Rai's mom in the kitchen garden.

The first step was to collect the dried twigs from the garden and light a fire inside the stove. While Rai's mom made delicious *bhakris* (roasted flatbread) on the top, we would pop in onions or sweet potatoes and the tamarind seeds into the hearth. By the time her cooking was done, the embers would still be glowing, and our precious stuff would get gently barbecued to perfection. Even Robby, the dog, loved roasted sweet potatoes in their jackets and would lie beside the *Chula*, and the fire would be reflected in his beautiful brown eyes as he gazed patiently into the glowing and dancing flames. At last, they would be done, and we used another twig to scrounge around in the hot ashes for our precious goodies. To us—and to Robby—the sweet, juicy roasted onions, the smoky sweet potatoes, and the hard, tasteless, yet addictive roasted tamarind seeds were as good as ambrosia!

It wasn't just tamarind, which was on the grab-and-go list of us school buddies; one of my classmates, who lived just across the road from the school, had a lush green Star gooseberry tree in her garden. This particular gooseberry isn't as tart as the regular one. The fruit is smaller, a beautiful yellow when ripe and a mix of sweet and sour. We all loved them. When the fruit was in season, she would bring a few with her to school, but on the days she did not, some of us would go to her house and collect the fruit during recess. We shouldn't have been off the school premises during school hours, but then there was no wall or fence to actually cross. So, technically, we weren't breaking any school rules (fingers crossed behind my back!). We would suck on these little fruits and put some for the road in our skirt pockets.

There was also an occasional almond tree whose ripe, red fruit would be strewn below the tree. Easy pickings, even if a little bruised. This fruit also had a sweet and sour taste but had a lot of fibre, making it a little difficult to eat, but then, what's a little fibre for daring explorers? The horde of langurs that resided in the area appreciated them equally, and you would often find them perched on nearby rooftops munching on them and scattering leftovers in the garden below making quite a mess. After all, they are related to us and cousins have quite a bit in common!

There were also *Jamun* or the Indian blackberry trees for which, again, there was competition between the arboreal monkeys and us cheeky monkeys. This fruit is quite delicate and colours the lips and tongue with its dark, inky-purple colour. There was no way you could hide the fact that you had sneaked off to eat *jamun* when you had actually been sent on an errand!

There were also *Ber* or Jujube trees that were quite prolific and didn't have many takers for the sweet-sour fruit because of the sharp thorns. The birds were quite fond of it, but after all, their appetites WERE birdlike and so there was plenty of it left over for us. There was a particularly big plant in our neighbour's garden. These folks were easy-going and did not particularly care for either the wild fruits or gardening and were happy to let us kids try our luck at getting them with just a casual warning to watch out for the resident cobra! Fortunately for us, snakes are not very keen on joining a noisy bunch of kids, especially on a hot afternoon and so we were never bothered by the serpent. There was also a huge *khirni* tree in the same garden. Its massive branches covered most of the kitchen garden in deep shade. This indigenous fruit is quite a rarity in the city markets nowadays. It is a tiny, yellow, oblong shape; the flesh is white and exudes a sticky, milky substance that is not very easily washed off. The squirrels, birds and monkeys all loved this fruit. So, when the tree was laden with this largess, there was heavy traffic in that particular garden, I can tell you, but as I said, the tree was huge, and the people were kind, so everyone got a fair share.

During the rainy season, the whole landscape got covered with short, stubby green grass and mushrooms sprouting here and there. These mushrooms were called the crow's umbrella—heaven knows why!—and weren't edible. One had to watch one's step on the mossy pathways as they were very slippery and claimed quite a few victims. My derriere and knees have painful memories of those days, I am sure! Then, there was a wide variety of wild flowers which bloomed in an assortment of colours, shapes and sizes. The Burr marigold was omnipresent, with its flat flowers held high on long stalks, swaying in the breeze. We would pluck a stalk and flick at the base of the flower. As this flower is bulbous and comparatively heavy, it would snap and fly off into the distance like a projectile! There were competitions to see who could flick it the farthest. I now think it was a waste of perfectly beautiful flowers!

Dandelions were also quite common. Their light and hairy seeds would fly off from their stalks and would float around silently like little cobwebby umbrellas. We would chase after them, and just as you thought you had caught one, a gust of wind would sweep it higher and out of your reach. One could imagine a miniature Mary Poppins hanging on to the seed and floating off to bring joy into the lives of some needy children.

The colony also had a well-stocked nursery which provided all the plants needed to beautify the public areas. If you had the right connections and the right people skills, both of which my mother had (the nursery manager's daughter was Shubhangi's classmate—practically family!), then you could also go and get a few rare plants for your garden. I used to accompany my mother on such occasions as, without her, the gates were firmly closed for us, figuratively and literally.

Behind these locked gates was a treasure trove of exotic plants. Flowers bloomed riotously along brick-laid paths around a big pool in which swam guppies and mollies. There were also goldfish, which flickered like actual gold as they swam in and out of the waving

Vallisneria and *Hydrilla* plants. Dragonflies swooped over the shimmering pool in colours as assorted as the flowers around them. I could have spent hours peering into the pool. But besides all these irresistible attractions, there was another exciting thing in the nursery, and that was the big huge tank, which was the water source for the entire colony. It soared up majestically from amongst all the plants on its strong legs and towered overhead. There was a pumping station below, and a small spiral staircase led up to the top. Just below the huge bulb, which contained the massive amount of water needed to maintain the township, though, were things which interested me more than the intriguing tank—there were three MASSIVE beehives! If you walked up the stairway a bit, you could see that what looked like a huge, solid black block was actually a living, writhing mass made up of thousands of bees crawling over each other, desperate to feed their young and fill the spongy hive with rich, delicious honey. The work of the bees was made easy considering that the source of their food was conveniently below them, and the plants certainly thrived from their attention. So, there we were! We had several colonies within a colony. How's that for live and let live?

While there was a wide variety of plants on the streets of the township, our garden had an equal variety of domesticated plants. I have already described our front garden and its residents earlier. Besides this, we had a

fantastic kitchen garden as well, thanks to the combined efforts of Rai and my parents. If we needed spinach for the salad, we just walked out and picked a fresh, crunchy handful. Feel like some onions? Well, go dig yourself a few! And how about some cucumber? Coming right up! We produced enough onions and potatoes to last us the whole year! They would be cleaned, dried and then spread out in the loft on jute bags. Then, there were sweet potatoes, carrots and radishes, and we even had peanuts one season.

I remember digging up a bunch of peanuts once, and a weird large insect crawled out; it had a bulbous head, short front legs with ridges and a dark brown body. It looked rather like a creature from outer space and a scary one at that! Rai got all panicky and told me to come away as this creature was 'the scorpion's aunt' and could bite deeply. Later, I learned that our alien was actually a mole cricket, generally subterranean. They can give quite a painful bite as they have quite strong jaws, but very rarely has such a case occurred, and even if it did, these crickets are not venomous. In fact, their short front legs, which are designed like a fingered shovel for tunnelling underground, might cause more discomfort than their jaws! These creatures can be herbivorous, carnivorous or omnivorous. The plant-eating variety does like nibbling on roots, so, possibly, I disturbed this particular specimen while he/she was peacefully eating lunch! I bet the encounter was as unsettling for it as it was for me.

On weekends, while most people went to the city for movies or eating out, you would find all of us out in the garden. My father would be hard at turning the soil with a grub hoe, and my mom would do the weeding with a sickle. Us kids and the dog would hang around, invariably getting in the way. I begged my mom for a small garden patch of my very own, and I remember I got it as well, but I soon lost interest when I realised how much work it actually entailed! Vinita and I loved to go and scrounge about in the upturned clayey soil. One day, we decided that I would make a kitchen set for her to play with using this very clay. We poured some water into a patch and happily squelched it around. After a couple of hours, we came up with things which looked kind of like utensils. We dried them out for a couple of days. It was suggested to us that they needed to be baked, and so we thought, why not bake them in the outdoor wood-burning stove. After a couple of hours, we were the proud owners of a blackened but tough playset of miniature kitchen utensils! I think that we had more fun making them than playing with them.

We had a bunch of banana trees as well, outside my parents' bedroom, which regularly bore huge, big tiers of the fruit. The trees created a sort of miniature grove, and in this grove, my father, loving dad that he was, set up a tent for us. I was an avid reader of Enid Blyton books, and I envied the way the Famous Five or Barney and the rest of the gang went off on camping trips at the drop of a hat without a care in the world! Those were not the days when you could procure a tent by ordering it on Amazon. So, after listening to my whining for days, my dad gave in and made me a huge tent from some old, green mosquito netting! It was beautiful and one of the best gifts ever!

Here, I would retreat in the afternoons with my books and comics, and, like the Secret Seven, I would sip lemonade from a *jalebi*-making bottle, which my mom let me have as it had a nozzle and hence convenient for sipping. Vinita would occasionally join me. It would invariably end up in us becoming a bit too noisy, and as a result, we would get a sound telling off from Mum because we had disturbed her much-needed afternoon nap! Although it contributed to a lot of disturbed afternoon siestas, the tent stayed up for a long time, serving as a hideout and clubhouse.

My dad had also made a volleyball court in the backyard with all the right markings (albeit not at the right distances), and here we spent many happy evenings as a family playing volleyball and ring tennis. The ball and the tennikoit ring would very often fly off at a tangent as we played with enthusiastic abandon with Robby barking madly and chasing them all over the court. They would very often end up in an arbour made for the cucumber or bitter gourd or would fly into the mini forest consisting of the pigeon pea shrubs! This patch was really pretty dense, and with the fallen leaves covering the ground, it would have been very hard indeed to spot the ring thank heavens for trusty Robby, who spotted it easily every time. The hard part was making him give it back to you!

Besides the bananas, we had other fruit trees like pomegranate, which hardly ever got a chance to ripen as we would pluck and eat them before that. Then we had a couple of papaya trees—well, technically speaking, shrubs—but they were very tall indeed and bore a large number of fruits. We all loved papayas; in fact, Robby loved them so much that he would even eat the bitter skin! Our papayas did not have many seeds, which, I am told, is the sign of a good papaya. What few we did get were coveted by friends and neighbours who would try to plant them for a good fruit yield. An interesting fact—papayas can be either hermaphrodites, females or males. The males do not bear fruit—only flowers. The things one learns without having to study in a textbook when one has a kitchen garden!

We also had a huge lime tree, which literally dripped with limes when the season was right. My mother made a huge quantity of lemonade preserve, jars of lime pickles and a kind of watery jam which was generously gifted left, right and centre and yet there would be tons left. I don't think any of our neighbours or friends ever had to go to a grocer for limes! This tree was a huge favourite of the weaver birds, who established a permanent colony on it. We were lucky enough to be able to see their nest-making skills up close—right from the first straw to the full suspended nest, the shape of which which reminds me of a snake charmer's flute.

These birds are just fantastic—we can't hope to do with our two hands what they can do with their beaks!! The tight, intricate nests which were suspended from twigs by just a few entwined blades of grass could not only support the chicks and the feeding parent but also withstand heavy storms. The parents were always carrying out maintenance work, so everything was shipshape. The nests were even reused during the next breeding season. The birds would arrive back, inspect the nest thoroughly, and clean it out from the inside, busily popping in and flying out to discard accumulated rubbish or weakened blades. Repairs would be done, and voila! There would soon be the cheep-cheep of baby weaver birds. The nests and noise would invariably attract predators; Robby would generally chase off cats, but snakes would come to try their luck at night. Actually, Robby wasn't afraid of snakes either, and I remember one time when he gave chase to the rockery cobra. I was totally panic-stricken and ran after him, yelling at him to stop. Must have been quite a sight—a snake slithering away at top speed, pursued by a panting pooch who was followed by a gibbering girl! We were quite sure that the snake would stop and strike, but fortunately for all of us, it escaped through the hedge where Robby could not follow.

But I digress; I was telling you about how the snake would try and get to the weaver-bird nestlings. The birds were obviously no fools; they hadn't chosen a prickly lime tree for no reason. But the poor snakes had to eat too and would try their luck, generally to no avail. After numerous futile attempts to circumvent the thorns, they would finally give up and slither off. Now, an enquiring mind (euphemism for a sceptic!) might wonder how on earth we knew when the snake arrived and when he left. Well, with numerous snakes around, we certainly knew the warning calls of the birds and the Indian palm squirrels which announced their presence. The weaver birds were no exception. If they started chirping raucously at night, it meant some serpent was trying its luck. They would keep up the cacophony till it gave up and went away. The lime tree was right between the courtyard and our bedroom, so that one could hear almost every chirp.

One day, while hanging out the washing in the courtyard, we discovered a serpentine specimen hidden behind some old boxes piled up in the corner. It must have been completely tuckered out from the efforts of trying to get to the birds and must have decided to rest in the nearest spot. Very sensibly, it most likely decided to try its luck the next day; quite logical, I would say, but

I don't think my mom quite saw it that way. She called my dad, and he, in turn, contacted a gentleman who was an expert snake catcher. He came, had a look and simply put his hand out, lifted the snake and put it into a sack! No fuss, no waste of time. It turned out that our invader was a nonvenomous rat snake. He was a beautiful, rich brown colour and must have been about three feet long. Rat snakes are called '*dhaman*' in that part of the country. They are regarded as a farmer's friend as their main prey is rats and mice, which account for a lot of destruction of the harvested grains. Over some tea and snacks (in India, when guests come, good manners dictate that they go away replete), the gentleman told us that he had done a lot of meditation and practice to have reached his level of confidence. It seemed he said special prayers everyday, which gave him his ability! Whatever it was, there was no doubt he was very good at this and was called upon whenever a snake was sighted.

There was an anecdote about his abilities. He had been called into the factory where my dad worked to remove a large snake coiled up behind some machinery. It seems he walked up to the snake very calmly and, as was his style, simply put out a hand, pulled it out from the hiding spot and put him in a cloth bag he had brought along. Everyone heaved a sigh of relief, but there was one smart aleck who commented that probably the snake wasn't venomous at all! This well and truly infuriated the snake catcher! He got hold of a cardboard or some such thing and poked the bag with it. Wham! The snake struck at the offending board. This board had fang marks and dripping venom! This shut up all the doubting Thomases! The good thing was these snakes were not harmed in any way. They were taken and released into safer neighbourhoods—for them as well as the humans.

The birds and mice in the kitchen garden attracted the attention of jackals as well. Come nightfall, you could see their silent silhouettes flitting in and out of the shrubs. Robby would get extremely excited and would want to be let out, but we were warned by the vet that jackals carried diseases which could be transferred to dogs. Also, there was always the fear that the skulk (which is the collective noun for jackals—I didn't know it either, till I looked it up!) would attack him. So, he was kept indoors, but the smart guy that he was, he would pretend to be in urgent need to relieve himself! What could one do? I would let him out from the front door, and he would saunter out and smell EVERY blade of grass while I leant against the wall, thinking of my warm bed but, at the same time, worrying about him. After he finished, I would plead with him to come back, and his response would be to bound joyfully around the corner of the house and into the backyard! Then, he would insist on being let in from the back entrance. So, the next time, I would let him out from the back door and tell him sternly to come in by the same door or else! But, of course, in 15 minutes, you could hear the scratching and whining at the front door! He was a very good dog, but every dog has his day, and Robby had to have his nights as well!

CHAPTER 6
DARING DALLIANCES

Our township was a veritable zoo by city standards, but for us, it was the norm to live alongside all sorts of creatures. During the rainy season, it really poured, and all the open spaces were flooded with water. The snakes and rats had no choice but to come out of their subterranean homes and find dry hiding places. We kids continued playing outside on the roads and in gardens—weather permitting—despite the reptilian exodus. All our parents told us to do was to keep a sharp lookout for and get out of the way of any slithering serpent, but that was about it! No hysterical paranoia. Our parents trusted us to spot danger and keep well away. It was all very matter-of-fact and part of our lives. So, when we saw huge six-foot cobras swimming across a submerged plot, all we would do was watch its graceful, undulating moments and then swap `snake tales': "You should have seen the one I saw in the canal!" or "The one I saw by the nursery was WAY bigger!" Humans had taken over the home of these poor snakes, so what could they to do but try and live in some garden or the other? In this struggle for survival, there were some casualties in the form of bites. Our township hospital was geared for such eventualities, so fortunately, there were no fatalities! On our nightly walks, Robby always warned us of any errant ophidian, but then snakes are not really looking for a confrontation with big mammals, and they would prudently remove themselves as far as possible. The chances of coming across a specimen were pretty high. Hence, every household in the colony considered a couple of powerful torches as a necessary investment.

Besides the snakes, there were other species of creatures which posed a bit of a danger to people. I remember vividly an incident which took place in our—I mean us girls'—bedroom; this room had a door which led out to the rear veranda and into the kitchen garden. My mom kept most weeds under control, and things were pretty much shipshape, so generally, nothing came in. But one day, as we were airing out our duvets in readiness for the approaching cool weather, a huge centipede fell out of one and started wriggling all over the room. You can imagine the sudden increase in the noise level! We sisters were panic-stricken and began clambering up on all available pieces of furniture while my mum frantically called my dad. The only possible weapon he could grab hold of was a stiff broom, which he brandished like a sword! Now, the centipede is a very agile creature, and its flat body could slip into the tiniest spaces. They have very effective mouth parts that can deliver a nasty and very painful bite which is rarely fatal to an adult human unless you have an allergic reaction. Still, a centipede is something you should give a wide berth to! And we were all rather young; Vinita would have been just about five years old, so certainly, my parents were not taking any chances! This particular specimen was fully grown with yellow legs and huge pincers (probably the Indian tiger centipede, which can grow to six inches in length). Each time Dad located it, it dashed away and hid elsewhere. There was total chaos in the room, but finally, my father managed to deliver a debilitating blow, and that was the end of the poor thing. I say a poor thing because I am quite sure it did not come into the room with any intention of hunting us down. Their diet consists of insects like cockroaches, locusts, etc., which we humans consider pests—so a good pest controller. But sadly, there was no way of catching it for a safe release at that particular time. It's a nocturnal creature and probably got into the room by mistake. The duvet offered warmth and safety, or so it probably thought. It was just a case of it being in the wrong place at the wrong time!

Having veritably grown up alongside snakes, I am not afraid of them; I do have a high degree of respect for them and tread carefully when one is around, but I won't run the other way if I see one. In my experience, they are as eager to avoid you as you are to get away from them! But there is one creature that I am terrified of! And I am very ashamed to say that it is the *Periplaneta Americana* or—as we know it—the BIG cockroach! Now, don't laugh! I know I am being silly, but there is a valid reason behind it—or so I like to think!

It all started when I was around eleven years old; I was taking a cool bath one hot evening, singing lustily and soaping myself vigorously, when out of the corner of my eye, I saw two big antennae waving in a friendly fashion through the drain. My singing croaked to a halt, and though I wasn't petrified of them in those days, I still did not want to share a bath with a cockroach. All seemed okay, as it did not seem too keen on coming out fully. I decided that I was clean enough and took my towel to wipe myself down. My intention of leaving seemed to have insulted the creature and so this massive specimen got out of the drain rapidly and, without warning, took flight STRAIGHT AT ME! Have you ever looked a cockroach in the face when it is in full flight, its wings spread akimbo, antennae waving madly, coming straight at you? Let me tell you, it is something right out of your worst nightmare! I can tell you I really screeched the place down—a banshee would have turned green with envy! I don't know how, but I managed to wrapped

something around myself and dashed out, still hollering as if someone was coming to murder me.

Since that day, I feel as if every cockroach I see wants to be my best buddy and would love to give me a hug! By the way, don't get any wrong ideas! I run a very clean house and have no cockroaches, but there are always other people who are more generous about sharing their living space than I am. Also, walk past garbage bins at night, and you will see a merry party of these particular insects enjoying the spoils of the day! They are quite social and like hanging out together. Some species even do collective decision-making, just like human families. If you think about it, theirs is a fantastic survival story. This species has been around for about 320 million years. They can be found over most of the planet, from the Arctic to the deserts! They are very hardy insects and could be likened to living fossils. They were there long before humans and are likely to be around after the human species eradicates itself!

Another species dating back from ancient times is the lizard. As I said, our garden had a wide variety of trees, creepers and bushes. An ideal habitat for these reptiles. We had the garden lizards who bobbed their heads at you with raised crests from their perches in the trees or on walls, we had geckoes that looked like miniature crocodiles with their flattened bodies and golden eyes, and hiding under all the leaf litter were the skinks with their sleek, gleaming bodies and beautiful snakelike movement. They were all present in large numbers in the garden, and territorial fights broke out every now and again. The beautiful *Madhumalti* or honeysuckle creeper on the veranda was an extremely desirable residence for the garden lizards because of the moths and ants it attracted, so there were always a few of them scampering around in its green fronds. This grew right by the main steps of the veranda, which was a favourite spot of ours to hang around as one could chat with passing neighbours while playing hopscotch on the driveway.

Vinita was jumping up and down the steps, and my parents were admiring the effect the setting sun had on the glorious roses and the colourful dahlias. It was a typical peaceful scene that was ripped apart suddenly by my siblings' screams. Upon being asked, she refused to say what the matter was and just clawed at her dress, wailing loudly. My parents went into panic mode, assuming a snake had got under her dress, and so, my father did the only thing he could—he ripped open the beautiful dress my mom had made for my sis, expecting to see a snake slither out. I cannot imagine what thoughts must have gone through his mind! But what fell out was a *Calotes versicolor*, which scrambled back up the creeper from whence it had fallen—most likely during a territorial fight—into my sister's frock! Everyone drew huge sighs of relief, including the said lizard, I imagine. After a bit of cajoling and loads of cuddles, baby Vinita also calmed down. Except for a few superficial scratch marks caused by the lizard's claws when it had desperately tried to climb out of the folds of the dress, she was unscathed.

Just a road away was the township's multi-purpose stadium. It was a big ground with a seating area that was used for all kinds of purposes: cricket matches, school sports days and national days. It was also the venue for funfairs and gatherings associated with seasonal festivals. Most of the time, it was just a massive empty expanse for us kids to run about or then there were those parents who struggled to teach their kids the complicated art of keeping your balance while riding a bicycle. It was very common to see red, perspiring adults chasing after shaky bicycles ridden by nervous kids weaving through the tracks on the ground as they struggled to remain upright.

On the fringes of the ground, where the weeds fought to slowly reclaim the land, there were nesting lapwings. These elegant birds are past masters at camouflaging their eggs! They would lay their eggs amidst a few pieces of dried dung. The colour of the eggs matched the colour of dried dung perfectly so that even if you stood over a nest, sometimes you couldn't spot the eggs. The lapwings are also very good at protecting their nest and its contents from potential egg hunters by pretending to be injured and luring them away. The predator is fooled into thinking that a nice, plump, injured bird is going to be easy pickings, so why bother with mere eggs? Once a good distance has been put between the nest and the hunter, the lapwing makes a miraculous recovery and flies off, and the location of the nest is still a well-kept secret! Now, that is parental love for you—risking your own life for the sake of your offspring!

But where did this dung come from? Well, there were a couple of villages nearby and sometimes, the villagers took advantage of the lax attitude of the authorities and sneaked their livestock onto the ground for grazing. So, there would be days when we had sheep and goats ambling around through the grass, and on other days, you would find a few donkeys with their heads down, busily cropping the turf; if you approached them, they would toss their heads, snort and canter off to a safer distance from where they would eye you accusingly from under their beautiful, long lashes! Occasionally, there would be a herd of cows and buffaloes moving about ponderously. They would watch you with disdainful eyes, jaws moving rhythmically as if they owned the land and you were the one trespassing! Most of these encounters with the bovine species were quite uneventful, but there was one occasion when it seemed to me that we would be far better off locked in a room with a snake than a supposedly domestic animal!

Vinita was a bit under the weather, so my mom decided we needed to make a trip to the hospital. The quickest way there was to cut across the stadium, so my mum picked her up, and I went along for company. We started trudging across the big ground. Now, on that particular day, three buffaloes were grazing on the ground. We ignored them and continued making our way across the ground. For some reason, one of the buffaloes saw red (I was indeed wearing a reddish frock, but cattle are supposed to be colourblind, so that was an intended pun!) and decided we needed to be chased off! The next few moments were terrifying, to say the least! Have you ever seen people running for their lives in the bull-running festivals in Spain? That's exactly how we felt when the buffalo charged us with its snorting, flared nostrils and horns held low. It was then that I realised that cattle, despite their bulky body, are agile and can run pretty fast! I was absolutely terrified, and my mom, the poor lady, hung on to my baby sister, who was probably enjoying the unexpected dash and, at the same time, tried to guide me away from the buffalo. It must have been quite a sight: a lady with a bouncing kid on her hip running helter-skelter with her sari flapping madly, a screaming kid trying to keep up and a thundering buffalo at their heels! In retrospect, it must have been a hilarious spectacle, but we were extremely panic-stricken at that moment and totally failed to find any humour in the situation! We must have run for a good fifteen to twenty metres before the buffalo's ego was satisfied, and it came to a halt. But after that day, whenever I spotted any cattle grazing on the ground, I went to the hospital the really long way round!

To reach the above-mentioned hospital, we had to cross a small metal bridge over the canal just beyond the ground. This was the very same canal that was meant to channel the excess water from the nearby village lake to safer areas. The times when there was water flowing through it, I would spend hours peering into the swirling murky waters, hoping to spot some interesting aquatic life. In the dry season, there was just vegetation—small shrubs, some grass and the occasional mice. This dry canal was used as a sort of freeway by a couple of monitor lizards. These animals are very shy, and even the slightest vibration set them off on a crazed lopping run, their long, heavy tails swinging wildly behind them. It was amazing to see these creatures in the natural environment, but later, when a petrochemical plant built its colony beside ours, these poor lizards disappeared. I like to think they found a better place for hunting and raising their young.

A lot of the people I meet tell me that they are scared of dogs or cats because they have been bitten at some point in their life. Well, I don't agree that this can be the sole cause. Most people involved in animal rescue have, at some point or the other, been bitten to a greater or lesser degree by the very individual they are trying to rescue. That is because the animal is absolutely terrified and cannot distinguish a friend from a foe in its panic-stricken state. I was in the tenth grade when it happened to me for the first time: I was at home studying at my desk by the window when suddenly I heard a pup whimpering in distress. I have never been able to ignore any animal in need of help which I come across. So, like a female Don Quixote, off I went in search of the pup. I followed the whines to a house outside where a young boy was pulling on the tail of a pup who was barely a month old. The mother was a stray and was fed by the boy's family. But I didn't feel that that gave them the right to manhandle the pups, so I took the pup from the kid and started lecturing him about the way he was treating the poor thing; from the corner of my eye, I saw its mother slinking up to me, and before I knew it, she bit me hard on my hand and ran off. She probably thought that I was the one who had been bothering the pup. I was so stunned and hurt by her action that I hardly felt the pain, and as I made my way home, dripping blood along the way, my eyes were just full of tears with the unfairness of it all. On top of it, my dad gave me a good, LONG lecture for doing such a foolish thing.

Strays in India aren't inoculated against rabies, and every year, there are a few human casualties as a result of rabid dog bites. My parents were naturally worried that I would soon start foaming at the mouth. So, I was rushed to the hospital. The lecture continued all the way there, along with an in-depth description of the agony I would have to suffer from the course of the anti-rabies injections I was now likely to get. The inconvenience of having to take me up and down to the hospital for the duration of the course and my total inconsideration in getting bitten was also pointed out to me! Fortunately for me, the doctor gave me just an anti-tetanus shot and yet *another* lecture on my thoughtless behaviour. The doctors were all a part of our local community and knew our parents socially. Hence, they thought nothing of taking such liberties. He just told us to keep a watch on the bitch (absolutely no pun intended!). If she was still in good health after a couple of weeks, there was no need for the anti-rabies injections. Phew! Fortunately for me *AND* the bitch, we were both perfectly ok even after the required period!

I bear scars to date on my arm where three canine teeth sank deep into my flesh, but even after that incident, my love for animals did not get affected. I perfectly understood the emotions which made the bitch react the way she did. Wouldn't a human mom, too, lash out at a stranger holding her crying baby? The worry-induced parental reprimands probably caused more of an impact on me than the bite!

And talking of concern for dependents, I recollect the lengths to which our parents and teachers went to keep us safe during the time our country was in combat with a neighbour. I was around seven or eight at the time, an age where the words 'war' and 'conflict' did not really percolate into my consciousness.

The refinery where my father and all other bread-earners residing in the township worked was under a serious threat of being bombarded by planes. An 'umbrella' of protection was created by installing anti-aircraft guns around the perimeter of the refinery. All windows of all the colony buildings—residential, school and official—were covered with dark paper from inside to reduce the amount of illumination which could give away the location of the colony to any enemy fighter jets. Warning sirens were installed. All the residents had been taught the basic techniques of self-preservation, even if we were outside on the roads. As I recollect, if the sirens went off while on the way to and fro from school, we were supposed to lie down on the road face-down and keep our ears covered in order to protect ourselves from the possible blast and shrapnel. This aspect gave an illicit thrill to us kids, and we eagerly awaited an opportunity to be able to act in this depraved manner. Unfortunately for me (and fortunately for my parent's peace of mind), I never got the chance!

There were practice sessions as well so that people would do it instinctively. These sessions took place at school as well. I remember distinctly that, being too young to understand the seriousness of the situation, we students had quite a blast—excuse the P.J.!—each time the sirens went off: firstly, it meant time off from studying—a huge plus point of the war in our naive eyes—and secondly, we seemed to get to act in the most undisciplined, unschool-like way! As soon as the sirens went off, we kids had to dive down under our desks and cover our ears, just in case. Our teachers also had to squeeze down under their cumbersome, metallic desks—saris and all—and then they had the difficult task of trying to control a whole lot of giggling kids who were up to mischief under the desks. Tiffins were being opened; tic-tac-toe games were indulged in vociferously, much to our teacher's dismay and occasionally, the outside war would be brought into the classroom in a miniature version when arguments broke out about the knee space under the desks. That is when I guess the teacher felt most helpless: unable to leave her station and yet having to try and restore harmony. We kids were quite blasé about the whole thing. However, the poor teachers were aware of the gravity of the situation and were under tremendous stress as they were responsible for the safety of thirty-odd children.

If the sirens went off at night, which they did (no truces at night, unlike in the olden days, unfortunately!), then it was a whole new adventure! There were no bunkers around, so our 'cave/ bunker' was under my parents' metal beds. There was a thick rug laid out under it. There was also a big old-fashioned metal chest containing stuff deemed essential like torches, water bottles, biscuits, books and basic first aid. As soon as the alarms went off, my mom would rush into our bedroom to wake tai and me, and she would carry the still-sleeping baby Vinita. We would sleepily slide under the parental bed and lie around like scattered sticks. Initially, when the whole thing was new, we used to be agog with excitement and would chatter nineteen to the dozen, but as the novelty wore off, it became just another tedious chore! My father occasionally had to rush off to the plant if there was an emergency, which caused my mother no end of worry! Fortunately for all of us and the countries involved, tensions were reduced, ruffled feathers were smoothened, and life became normal once more.

CHAPTER 7

ARBOREAL AMOURS

*I*f I have perchance conveyed the impression that there was a daily dramatic encounter with some extraordinary species of animal or the other, that wasn't my intention. We were just a regular set of people living ordinary lives. Alongside the few uncommon species of animals we came across, our township had all the typical creatures one would expect to find in the countryside: the butterflies, house lizards, ants, beetles, cockroaches, crows, sparrows—you get the picture! But even in these ordinary creatures, one could have an occasional extraordinary story.

We had a pair of sparrows who had their permanent home in the pelmet of our dining room window curtains. Sparrow nests are an untidy mass of grass which sheds like a hairy dog in summer! It was in a state of constant disrepair. So, the pair would be forever trying to patch it up and would bring numerous grass blades into the dining room, dropping at least seventy percent of them. My mom got fed up with having a straw-festooned dining room and suggested a box. My dad took a shoebox, cut out one side and stuck it under the pelmet. The sparrows were thrilled with it, and so was Mom—no more straw on the floor!

Soon, we heard the cheep-cheep of baby sparrows and observed them as they stuck their bald heads and gaping maws out of the nest to be fed by their diligent and adoring parents. A constant supply of food was brought in. To help the parents out, we kept some rice, chapati pieces and water on the window ledge. These were mostly consumed by the parents themselves, but we like to think it did reduce their burden just a bit. The fledglings grew, and we observed them as they took their first tentative flying lessons on the veranda just outside the window. They were very soon proficient in the art and would follow their parents around from branch to branch, harassing them till they succumbed to their demands and fed them. Then, they would sit replete with a self-satisfied expression on their faces. Soon, the nest was empty, and the cock and hen were free to romance once again. Sure enough, in a few days, we could see the pair taking turns to hatch the new lot of eggs in the same nest in the shoe box. And so, it continued: one lot hatched, was raised conscientiously and then flew off, and the next lot started. It was like having pet sparrows—they were very used to us, as we to them. We were soon to realise that these birds are big-hearted and adaptable to situations as well.

We were on a trip to the local museum—a favourite haunt of ours as it was also in the same complex as the zoo *AND* had an ice cream parlour next to it! What more could a nature-loving family want on a day out? We ambled past the Chinese exhibit, dawdled over old whale bones and were about to enter the art gallery. The museum building was built in colonial times and is a majestic structure of turrets, stone floors and very high ceilings. In one corner of the ceiling, next to the entrance of the art gallery, was a sparrow nest, and it was as ramshackle as a sparrow's nest can be. Five nestlings had fallen through a hole in the nest and had miraculously survived the twenty-foot fall. But there was no way we could climb up and deposit them back in their home. We searched for ladders, but no help was forthcoming, so we did the only sensible thing we could do—we took them home!

The nestlings were too small for us to be able to raise, so my dad climbed up on a chair and put them into the nest in the pelmet. We knew they had just laid a batch of eggs and hoped that they would look after this lot as well. And adopt them, they did! They immediately started on the feeding-cleaning routine. Their own eggs were sadly discarded, I think—probably too many mouths to feed. I had half expected them to peck the strange chicks to death, but they did no such thing! They fed and raised the stray lot as their very own, though I am sure they realised that they weren't their own flesh and blood. Later on, the poor male lost his life to a ceiling fan, and another male took over the duties of a loving father, allowing the sparrow population in our dining room to continue thriving. How many humans would be able to display the same generosity as these sparrows had exhibited, I wonder!

As I keep stating, our colony was very green with all sorts of trees and shrubs, so this was an ideal habitat for the Indian palm squirrel. You could see them everywhere: bounding along on the lawns, clambering up trees, sitting on their haunches in the middle of the roads, staring at you with quivering moustaches and twitching noses. They were very alert creatures and warned the entire neighbourhood of the presence of any predator. Anytime you heard the shrill 'ch-ch-ch' sound, the first thing to do was to look hurriedly around yourself to make sure that there was no snake in your vicinity, and after heaving a sigh of relief, you looked for the crow or *koel* who might be hiding in a tree hoping to snack on some eggs from a nest. They were really cute creatures with their soft greyish brown bodies and the white and black stripes down their back. They had an endearing way of sitting up on their haunches to survey the surroundings, their tails held up high over their backs, and at the slightest sign of danger, they would start chirping and would flick their tails vigorously as if trying to beat out a code on a drum.

We had quite a few palm squirrel nests up in trees—big, messy-looking affairs which were made from anything which was remotely soft, from bunches of cotton pulled out from mattresses being aired to dried-up grass, bits of wool, dog hair, pieces of cloth and a favourite was unravelled coir! In those environmentally friendly days, most of the rope used in gardening and for other sundry purposes was coconut coir rope. This they would cut with their razor-sharp incisors, bunch up in their mouth and bound off to their nests. Generally, these nests would be located high up in the branches or in the hollows of old trees where it wasn't easy for the predators to climb. Even so, I have seen a snake coil its way up diligently towards a nest while the parent squirrels went crazy with fear for their young ones.

When a snake was involved, even an enemy could become a saviour. Generally, the snake would be chased away by crows who are not above making a quick snack of a young squirrel themselves if the opportunity presents itself! One stormy night, a nest in our casuarina tree fell down. In it were three babies whose eyes had not even opened—little pink and bald creatures who were all head! We had no experience with squirrels, and in those days of no internet, there was no way of finding out. Our vet lived in the city far away and made just a few trips a year for our dog's vaccination. All we knew was that they needed nourishment. We had no dropper or bottle with a teat tiny enough for their mouths. So, my dad decided to take some cotton, dip it in milk and trickle it down their mouth. It was difficult, but it seemed to do the trick. Unfortunately, we did not know that the babies needed to be stimulated to pass urine and defecate. By the time we learnt about this, we sadly lost two of them to compacted bowels! To date, I feel miserable about this. I wouldn't have mentioned this sad incident here if I hadn't thought that it could serve to help other rescuers. But one did survive and brought much joy to us!

We had named him Chintoo. He was quite the hyperactive little boy. The words 'walk 'or 'amble' were missing from his dictionary. He would just dash around madly as if he was falling behind in a busy schedule. He loved riding on our shoulders as it gave him a great vantage point! His other favourite pastime was running up and down curtains. Our windows were now mostly closed for his protection, so that was no problem. He would climb up high into the pelmet and peek out at us naughtily, daring us to try and grab him. The phrase 'bright-eyed and bushy-tailed' could have been made to describe him!

But we, too, had a trick up our sleeves; all we had to do was open the sugar tin noisily, and before you could put the lid down, Chintoo was in the tin! He was thoroughly addicted to sugar and would sit in the tin with the tiny crystals held in his hand, popping a few at

a time into his mouth, chewing vigorously and noisily, all the while keeping his bright eyes trained on you, whiskers twitching in excitement. If you tried to remove him from the tin, he would grab hold of the edge so hard that if you pulled on him, the tin would get dragged as well! He also loved eating Chapatis. My mom would make some for lunch, and they would be placed in a special round container with a tight lid. Chintoo always joined us for lunch and was eager to try everything. To keep him out of our plate, we would give him scraps on the side and eat quickly before he finished his meal. He would take a piece of chapati and nibble on it, turning it round and round like the steering wheel of a car turning only in one direction. He would stuff as much food as he could and as fast as possible in his little cheeks in case the rest of us finished it all!

After the meal was over and stuff cleared away, the leftover chapatis would be in their steel container on the table, and all of us, squirrel included, would shift to the bedroom—us kids to do our homework (with numerous breaks to take a quick peek at the latest escapades of Phantom or Tintin) and Chintoo to take a nice siesta. On one such occasion, while we were 'engrossed' in schoolwork, we heard a loud clatter from the dining room. Petrified that a cat had got into the house and fearing the worst for Chintoo, we raced to the dining room. Lo behold, the culprit was caught red-handed! Chintoo had somehow, with his dexterous little paws, managed to take off the lid of the chapati tin, which was at least ten times his size and almost as many times heavier than him. The lid had rolled off the table and fallen down, causing the clatter, but it did not seem to have fazed Master Chintoo in the least bit! He had jumped right into the tin and was sitting on the chapattis, busily munching on a piece with an expression of pure delight on his face. My mom would get indignant with his shenanigans—and rightly so—but we always had a good laugh afterwards. He was still rather tiny, so we had to be really careful not to sit on him by mistake. He had a wickerwork basket with a lid in which he slept, which was kept locked. However, if he was in an active mood, you had to be very careful about securing the lid properly, or else he would escape by squeezing out under it.

My dad's brother lived in Ahmedabad, a city about a hundred-odd kilometres away from Vadodara. His two children—a boy named Vivek and a younger girl named Himangi—were around our age, so we all got on like a house on fire. They would visit us often and vice versa. Chintoo was very much part of all household activities, and when we went on a trip to visit them, he went with us. He would be put inside his basket, and off we would go. Chintoo would happily clamber out of his basket and roam all over the car and us, uncaringly digging his tiny yet sharp claws into our skin until, for his safety and ours, he was firmly locked up till we reached our destination. We had to weigh down the basket lid, or else he would manage to create a gap and squeeze out as easily as a snake! While we were there, one of Vivek's friends came over.

We introduced Chintoo to him. Chintoo was thoroughly pleased to have made a new acquaintance: '*Su amigo, mi amigo!*' he seemed to say. He was keen to explore said 'friend' thoroughly. But the boy took askance at a squirrel going under his shirt—sharp claws, tickly whiskers—not exactly a soothing experience, especially for a newly initiated animal carer! So, with the greatest reluctance, as evidenced by claw marks in the fabric where Chintoo had hung on, hoping to convince everyone that all was good, he had to retire back into his basket.

He was naturally curious and would poke around in blankets and books. The sugar tin was the only thing that could make him leave his hiding spot. But he was getting older and a little aggressive. I suppose he was yearning for his own kind. Maybe this was the reason he ran away. I can't remember how, but one day, Chintoo escaped into the garden and bounded into some tall grass. We followed hot on his heels and looked for him everywhere, but to no avail! After this, we imagined that each squirrel who came into our yard looked like him, and we would do our best to get near it with no luck. All we could hope for was that he was safe wherever he was and had a squirrel family of his own.

CHAPTER 8

RANDOM REMINISCENCES

*S*trangely enough, despite the vast variety of life around us, most other people we knew did not seem to be going ga-ga over it like us. I would stop in mid-sentence to stare after a butterfly or halt in mid-stride to peer into a puddle, but my friends seemed to get a bit fidgety with all these interruptions. Even our vet seemed very prosaic and unemotional whenever we excitedly tried to share our critter stories. So, meeting anyone who showed signs of being an animal lover was a great pleasure. Common hobbies can easily cross over barriers of language and culture. This was borne upon us in many ways and instances during our stay in the township.

Our house was at one edge of the colony. When we first moved into it, there were big open spaces beyond our garden which led to farmland further on. Sadly, 'progress' does not stop, and the fields and wild areas were cleared to make way for yet another township meant for the employees of a petrochemical plant being set up nearby. While the construction was ongoing, technical experts from around the world were brought in to help the local talent. There were people from Germany and also from Japan. Their accommodation was just behind our row of houses. These folks did their shopping at the commercial centre in our colony as we had better amenities and choices. They were allowed access through a small gate situated one house away from ours.

As I mentioned earlier, our garden was a prize-winning one thanks to my mother's avid gardening interest. This attracted the attention of a Mrs Fitzek and a Mrs Steinchen from Germany, who were keen gardeners themselves. They popped in once to admire the garden, and then it became quite a routine; they would stop by on the way to the shops for a cup of tea, and the ladies would take a round in the garden, conversing all the while in broken English as none of them had a good grasp of the language. In return, we were also invited for tea to their homes where, for the first time, I sampled beautiful German baked goodies like their milk rolls, donuts, sweet rolls and a variety of cakes. Their house smelt perfectly divine on a baking day! But besides the lovely goodies, there was an added attraction at the Steinchen's home: their black poodle. They were a senior couple, and there was no one back home to look after the dog, so they had brought it (I would generally not refer to a dog as 'it' but I am unable to remember the gender, so decided to be politically accurate!) over with them to India. We were thoroughly impressed by their commitment towards the little creature. It was the apple of their eye and had loads of toys, and—this truly amazed me at the time—they had an inflatable pool for the dog! They were worried about the heat affecting the dog, who was black, hairy and used to a cold climate. So, on hot days, the pool used to be filled, and the dog would splash around happily in it, much to our envy!

Then, there was the encounter with some Japanese folks. They were also part of a team which was on deputation to help with the installation of the new petrochemical plant. Their balcony looked out over our backyard. On one occasion, the Ahmedabad cousins were visiting us, and as usual, the adults had shooed us out to play so that we kept out of the way of dinner preparations. All of us kids—including our German shepherd, Robby—enjoyed smoked sweet potatoes and onions. So, we headed for the backyard—most of us in our slips and shorts as scrounging around in the kitchen garden is most definitely detrimental to the state of good clothes! Some shrubs had just been weeded out, and we were told to use them as firewood. We made a big pile for a bonfire, stuffed it with the veggies and lit it. We hung

around chatting, singing lustily and occasionally chasing Robby around the yard.

All the time, we felt we were being observed. I looked up and saw a gentleman with a zoom lens standing on a balcony. I immediately pointed out this peeping tom to the others, and we all proceeded to make faces at the person who was so shamelessly invading our privacy. The poor man backed off indoors hurriedly, and we proceeded with our activity, the upshot of which was plump, smoke-flavoured sweet potatoes and caramelised, juicy onions which were sugar-sweet. The end result was a forgone conclusion: a bunch of thoroughly satiated kids and a replete dog who licked everybody's face and hands making sure that not a scrap went to waste!

We forgot all about the cameraman and the invasion of privacy until a few days later, when a gentleman dropped by and handed over a photo of us in our backyard. It seems the Japanese guys were curious about Indian families, and so had thought they could take a couple of photos of us as a sample for folks back home. Come to think of it, it makes us sound as if we were an endangered species in the forest, which should be recorded for posterity! But my parents, being the gracious people they were, decided to overlook the bad manners of the `foreigner` and very generously took us to pay them a house call, bearing a few goodies to make up for our facial antics. Shubhangi tai even discussed some aspects of Japan with them—she is very knowledgeable about a lot of things—and we came away hoping they had further insight into the real Indian psyche.

This dancing around in the yards and games of chasing or being chased by the dog was all done barefoot (come on, who had the time to go to the shoe rack and put on chappals? It was all on the spur-of-the-moment kind of thing!). Naturally, it was going to have consequences, and so it did! There was an Indian Gum Arabic tree growing just outside our backyard. The bark of this tree is supposed to be very good for massaging the gums and the teeth. Hence, the small twigs are chewed on by villagers as a natural disposable toothbrush. I, too, have given it a shot; the bark is slightly bitter and has a lot of fibre, which does an excellent job of cleaning the teeth. Plus, the rhythmic chewing motion (rather like a cow chewing cud!) is good for the jaws and gums. Rai's mom used to prune the tree and collect a bundle of twigs on a regular basis making sure to remove the big white thorns which adorn this tree. They have a dark tip and look rather like thin bones bleached in the sun. They do a stunning job of protecting the plant from most grazing animals and from little girls who may unintentionally run into them!

One day, I managed to step on one of the twigs which had fallen unnoticed. As is wont with kids, I ignored the pain for as many days as I could until it became unbearable to put my foot down! My heel was an angry red colour and really turgid. My father finally decided to get the thorn out, and no amount of pleading could persuade him otherwise. Some jaggery was heated up, and the gooey mess was applied to my heel. Now, that sounded rather straightforward, but I am ashamed to say that I was far from stoic. No stiff upper lip for me: my vocal cords were being efficiently used for screaming and yelling as the hot jaggery burned my already VERY sore heel! This process was meant to draw out the thorn, which was deeply embedded. My sister and mother held me down as I created the most awful ruckus while my father gently squeezed my heel. The jaggery did its trick; the heat caused the pus-filled abscess to burst, and the pus poured out—an extremely gross but very necessary purging. Once the wound was cleaned, my Dad gave a little squeeze, and the thorn shot out of it like a miniature rocket! All of us heaved a sigh of relief—me because it indicated an end to my ordeal and the intense throbbing pain which had dramatically disappeared—and the others because my caterwauling had stopped! For a few days after this, I assiduously put on my chappals each time I went into the garden, but soon, the painful memories faded, and I was back to my barefoot and careless romps!

Speaking of careless romps, an activity I was fond of (in those days) was climbing, be it trees or walls. As the reader may recollect, I had a disastrous experience in my childhood attempting to scale one wall and, sadly, ditto experience with trees as well! We had a drumstick or Moringa tree in the kitchen garden. This tree is quite soft and not really fit for climbing, but I wasn't going to let a little detail like that bother me! I used its branches as a perch to lean over and pluck pomegranates from the shrub which was next to it. Fortunately, the moringa tree wasn't very tall, so out of the many falls I had, I sustained only one tailbone fracture, which was not discovered till about ten years ago. So, it doesn't count!

A very nice courtyard connected my parents' bedroom and the guest room, which had a lovely, big, family-sized wooden swing. This space was enclosed from three sides and had a wide stone parapet at one end which opened onto the rockery side of the garden. There was a huge coral jasmine (*Parijat*) shrub as well as a night-blooming jasmine shrub, which had been planted strategically just along the parapet so that at night, the scent wafted into the bedrooms. Many are the nights we spent singing and swinging while munching on my dad's famous chapati omelette sandwiches. Often, we would all sit in the dark, with just the starlight bouncing off the walls while the trees and plants would cast eerie shadows and whisper in the breeze, giving a whole other-worldly feel while he regaled us with stories, the strong scent of the jasmines wafting around—rather like a scene from *One Thousand and One Nights* except for the fact that our Scheherazade was a male, moustachioed version!

Bruce Lee movies were one of my favourites in those days; all his elegant martial arts skills impressed my young mind. I was positive that I had it in me to do stunts equally well! The courtyard parapet would have been a laughable hiccup for him! I decided that if he could scale walls effortlessly, then so could I! And so began my numerous attempts at doing so. I tried to execute each attempt as gracefully as possible. The increasing number of scrapes and cuts on my knees and shins bore witness to my diligent efforts! One fine afternoon, something on the Coral jasmine plant triggered an allergic reaction in me, and I broke out in hives. I wasn't very bothered as I was in no pain, just itchy. In just an hour or so, I looked like the superhero 'The Thing'! My mom panicked and dragged me to the hospital, where I was prescribed antihistamines. After that day, though, all stunts in the courtyard were categorically banned!

I had always liked to imagine that there was a Dr. Dolittle hidden in me somewhere. I would try to imitate the birds around me or, being an avid reader of science fiction, try my (non-existent) skills of telepathy on unsuspecting butterflies fluttering by innocently or the palm squirrels who leapt around in the grass, all to no avail. Alas, they remained blissfully unaware of my efforts. Robbie, though, understood me and my nuances perfectly, but he didn't count because he understood my mother tongue very well. I had the sneaking feeling that perhaps his command of it was better than mine! But I never gave up hope!

I was sitting by our garden gate one day, playing in the gravel, when suddenly, a flock of silverbills flew down near me and started chirping and pecking around. They were some of the sweetest little birds I had seen with their small, greyish-brown, neat bodies and bright black eyes. I decided that this was the moment to try my bird whisperer skills, so I gently stretched out my hand, all the time trying to talk 'silverbill.' After cocking their heads to one side to give me disbelieving looks, the flock ignored me and carried on their pecking, but one of them came near and hopped onto my palm! I was astounded! I never imagined that a wild bird would trust me enough to come close—and here was one actually sitting on my palm! I was so amazed that I sat still and held my breath for fear of scaring the tiny thing. The little thing hopped off in a few seconds and re-joined his feathered brethren. Either the bird had been a juvenile one who hadn't been taught about the big, bad humans, or it was just too trusting. But what I had hoped for happened!

I no longer fantasise about being Dr Dolittle. Nonetheless, I do hope that I can have a better understanding of the behaviour of the other creatures in nature and can, in some way, create a two-way communication with them. And whether or not we understand animal/bird language, the fact that they understand us humans splendidly is something I firmly believe. This was made abundantly clear to us when a group of us kids visited the zoo.

During one summer vacation, some cousins from my maternal side were visiting the city, and the grownups decided that a good way of entertaining us would be a trip to the local zoo. The fact that the zoo premises had a lovely ice cream outlet (as I have mentioned rather gluttonously earlier) was an added attraction. So, off we all went. The first stop was the big cat section. These felids were in big cages, all cordoned off for the safety of the public. But one of my cousins simply couldn't resist teasing the animals—despite the rest of us telling him off. Mind you, all of us cousins are animal lovers through and through, but I guess he was just feeling excited about being away from grownups for a bit.

From the big cat section, we proceeded to the bird section, arguing all the way about the need to respect the live exhibits. This cousin was now in hyper mode and imitated each bird as we passed the cages, causing them to stop and stare after us in a perplexed fashion. Then came the turn of the primates. Here, too, the cousinly shenanigans continued. He peered into each cage and made loud, raucous sounds accompanied by the most awful facial distortions! The vervet monkeys and rhesus macaques gave him surprised stares and then literally turned their back on him and his rude gestures. This just egged him on, and by the time we reached the langur cage, cousin dear had decided he had to get a better reaction. So, he leant over the barricade and almost stuck his face into the bars, all the time doing a great imitation of a howler monkey with a stomach ache! The langurs gave him surprised looks. Then, he began hopping around and scratching his stomach in what he fondly thought was typical monkey fashion. The langurs looked insulted and decided they had had enough. One alpha male who was near the bars and who had gauged the distance correctly suddenly shot his arm out at full stretch and grabbed my cousin by his hair. For a while, there was a shocked silence, and then the silence was broken by my cousin's panicked shouts and—I must admit guiltily—our loud guffaws! I know we should have been concerned for his safety, but the sight of the langur clenching the hair of its teasing tormentor calmly with the most self-satisfied expression on its face was extremely funny. The fact that it was well deserved helped assuage our conscience. As there was a barrier of strong bars, there was no danger of bites, but it couldn't have been pleasant to have a wild animal attached to your hair, close enough to see all the big canines! Despite all his tugging and twisting, my cousin just couldn't get himself free. Finally, after discreetly wiping our tears of mirth and trying to replace our grins with expressions of concern, we tried to think up ways of getting the langur to release its grip. There were no keepers in the vicinity, so it was entirely up to us. One of the others had the brilliant idea of giving a banana to the vengeful primate. This tactic worked. Once the langur saw the banana, he seemed to assess the pros and cons of the situation. He reluctantly let go of the hair to set about the infinitely more rewarding task of peeling and devouring the banana. My young kinsman was vastly relieved, and we decided we deserved some refreshing ice cream to help us recuperate from the incident. We licked our ices with great gusto and loud, exaggerated slurps in order to cover our uncontrollable giggles and spare cousinly blushes as we recollected the incident!

The whole episode helped to reaffirm my belief that the other creatures of God have a good understanding of human behaviour and are much wiser than we give them credit for.

CHAPTER 9
FAMILY FESTIVITIES

*I*n India, we are a festive lot. Give us the slightest excuse, and we will go all out and make merry. Celebrations are family times—an excuse for a gargantuan get-together of the entire extended Indian family with first, second, even third cousins! Also, distant uncles and aunts—twice removed included! It is actually quite a blast! My mom's parents lived in the same city as us; hence, for us, visiting was quite convenient. On the maternal side, I had numerous maternal uncles, aunts, and a huge group of cousins. I particularly remember our gatherings at the ancestral home on the occasion of Ganesh Chaturthi which is the festival celebrating Lord Ganesh or the elephant God.

On this occasion, the entire clan descended on the city from wherever they resided. Most of them were put up in the mansion that my grandparents called home. The original building was like a miniature palace, complete with an imposing drawing room with a beautiful hand-painted ceiling and colourful glass chandeliers. Then came an inner courtyard with a pretty stone fountain in the middle, and this led into the house proper. There was also quite a big garden with a well; later, my uncle added a pond. There was also a huge family-sized swing in the main living room.

One of the favourite pastimes of us cousins was to pile onto the swing together and take huge big sings, belting out songs in a totally tuneless, uncoordinated way. I am sure one could have classified this cacophony as torture, but it kept us all out of the way of the busy adults, so they put up with it. One fine morning, though, the poor, misused and overworked swing simply gave up trying to support us; one moment, we were swinging away madly, throats sore with all the singing, and the next, we were scattered all over the living room like confetti. There was stunned silence for a few seconds, and then various hysterical aunts rushed to our aid like a set of homing missiles. Fortunately, except for a few scraped knees and elbows, we were all in one piece. Sadly, couldn't say the same about the swing, though. It was hanging pathetically by one end while the other end lay on the flagstones, completely detached from its anchoring! It had been a narrow escape, and our lame giggles were testimony to the fact that we realised how lucky we had been.

In those days, a grand house had to have a grand library. And it was indeed so in this case, as well! Old books lined the walls from ceiling to floor. Big huge volumes on every subject—from mythology to fiction, from tedious tomes to light-hearted joke books, from magazines to pamphlets—the library had it all. And the smell of it was simply divine! It was as if all the words poured out of the books and mixed up to create a unique scent! There were some real gems secreted away in nooks and crannies: old volumes of *The Condensed Reader's Digest* lay yellowing in one corner, while textbooks of Chemistry, Physics, and Zoology lay waiting to be poured over in another section. I glanced through Mahatma Gandhi's *The Story of My Experiments With Truth* perched in one corner of the bibliotheca, poured over *Learn German* booklets, flipped through stacks of *Span* magazines, and basically learned to love books in this very place. On the visits when the cousin gang was not around, Shubhangi tai and I would rush off to the library as soon as it was polite to do so and would be hidden away in its depths till someone came calling us for refreshments.

The maternal side of my family is also pretty animal crazy; there have always been dogs in the yard, a turtle in the well and fish in the pond. My mom told me that as kids, they even had a few deer, rabbits and cows. Add to that some visiting grandchildren, and it was a proper menagerie! The garden had three huge Ashoka trees, which were regular nesting places for egrets. The dark and dense green foliage of the trees seemed to turn into a moving, fluttering, white mass with the massive number of birds perched on them. Generally full white, these birds are speckled with bright yellow plumage during the breeding season.

During this time, the air was filled with their honking and wheezing, which they fondly imagined to be melodious love songs but were rather jarring to the human ear. The air reeked with the stench of massive amounts of droppings. You had to be careful not to pass under the trees; otherwise, you were sure to have a new pattern on your clothing! Egret nests are just a higgledy-piggledy heap of sticks. So inevitably, the odd eggs would fall and break, and sadly, quite a few chicks also met their end on the ground below. One year, a chick fell but managed to survive. My uncle picked it up and successfully raised it to adulthood. I remember how it followed him like a dog on the garden paths, stalking purposefully along behind him, pausing thoughtfully now and then to pull at some herbs. Its whitish round eyes gave it a mad look. It also had a disconcerting way of cocking its head to one side and giving you a piercing stare as if it thought you were a nice juicy grasshopper it could have for a snack. I was a little wary of the long yellow beak, which darted in a flash like a lance which had been stuck onto its head. I don't recollect exactly what happened to the bird later on, but

he was around for a pretty long time. On the whole, the egret colony thrived, and definitely, a lot more birds left at the end of the season than had arrived.

Then, there was my paternal side of the family. These grandparents lived far away in the state of Maharashtra. For the festival of Diwali, all the schools had a winter break, and we would pile into the car and drive off to celebrate this festival of lights with them: 'we' being my parents, us three sisters, my Ahmedabad uncle and aunt and my two cousins. The total came to four adults and five kids. I have absolutely no idea how we fit into our Ambassador car, along with a fortnight's worth of clothing and gifts; plus, the very essential goodies needed for three meals along the way! In those days, there were very few gas stations or rest areas on the way where one could pick up food, so we always packed loads of food. Five excited kids must have proved extremely nerve-racking for the adults, and the best way to keep us quiet was to ply us with food.

On D-day, we would get up early in the morning—that is, those of us who had managed to sleep despite the excitement. After a hurried wash, we would pile into the car around six o'clock in the morning. How my father managed to drive with two kids sitting on the lap of an adult next to him, I cannot fathom! Also, the rearview was totally blocked by a heap of bags! But thanks to his driving skills, we always made it to and fro every year without much problem.

Hunger pangs seemed to strike us even before we left the city limits, so lovely chutney sandwiches with homemade butter and boiled eggs would be passed around (to date, I have not been able to recreate that taste, try as I might!). Breakfast over, we would look out at the passing scenery that included occasional towns, numerous big and small rivers and lots of fields. A round of the quintessential *antakshari* (a kind of singalong game with teams) was a must—front seat versus the back seat folks, and we would all holler out songs lustily. Around midday, we would halt for lunch, generally by a shady spot near a river. The menu would be a nice dry curry with chapatis and a big bulb of raw onion. There would be some dessert as well—*sheera* (a sweet made out of semolina) or some *ladoos* pinched from the Diwali largesse—and then we would stretch our legs a bit before continuing onwards.

We had a favourite riverside spot where we generally stopped. There was a low cement bridge spanning the river at that particular spot. It was quite low because, generally, the flowing water could be described as more of a reluctant shallow stream than a river. But there was one time when the water level had risen sharply due to heavy rains, and the road had completely disappeared under a torrent of muddy, rushing water. We were rather in a quandary because the nearest detour was very far away, and we would have been unable to make it to our destination even by night. Hotels were as good as non-existent in the villages. But there was a tractor waiting to help out people in our situation. My dad decided to take a chance and cross to the other side. One end of a thick rope was tied to the tractor, and the other to the front end of our car. The sturdy tractor slowly and surely crossed over the bridge, dragging us behind. Dad was at the wheel, holding the car steady using a low gear as the water gleefully tried to push us over the edge. I remember the car felt like it was being dragged along with the water, and Dad had to struggle to control it, the engine groaning with effort. The rest of us sat still, holding our breaths—as if that would have helped! After what felt like an interminable amount of time, we reached the other bank and collectively expelled our breaths in one huge sigh!

Another year, the bridge had been totally washed away, and we crossed the river on a ferry with our car and a few people. It was my very first experience of being on a boat with vehicles. This ferry was basically a huge raft made of logs bound together with rope. I kept expecting us to sink anytime, and boy, I can tell you I was vastly relieved to put my feet on terra firma again.

These were just some of the unforgettable experiences we had on each trip we made to the family home, going up and down rolling hillocks, shouting out 'Ahoy, there' as loudly as we could like a bunch of drunken sailors from *ye olde world* as we approached a steep descent (don't know how it started but it was a tradition which never ceased to fill us with mirth) till at last we reached our destination with the last bit of faint light coming from the setting sun over the hillocks and painting everything red. We would jump out and be hugged by Grandpa and uncles. I would spy Smokey the dog through the milling adult legs and rush to greet him, and then there would be a mad dash to the washroom to relieve the pent-up feelings of the entire day, so to speak!

The ten-odd days we spent at my father's village created wonderful memories and strengthened the foundation of my love for animals—big and small. My Grandpa, or Bappa as we all called him, used to be a manager in a cotton gin. Put like that, it seems very mundane, but for us cousins, it was a heavenly place!

The residential accommodation—a typical rural cottage—was situated on the premises and was very basic and simple, to put it mildly. The kitchen was a low, warm room where we all sat on the floor to eat while my grandma made hot bhakri bread on a wood-burning Indian 'choola' or stove. This was a novelty for us and looked idyllic, but my mom and aunt, not being used to cooking on it, must have found it very difficult indeed! All the work had to be done cross-legged or on your haunches—cooking, washing up, sweeping, mopping, washing clothes—you get the idea!

There were rudimentary outhouses situated quite a distance away from the main house, so if you had the urge to relieve yourself after dark, it involved a torch-lit walk up a small path, and then you never knew who was waiting to greet you inside—frogs, house lizards or the omnipresent mosquitoes. On a stormy night, when the wind howled outside and the rain clattered on the roof tiles, waking you up, you inevitably felt like going to the bathroom; the wise thing to do was turn to your side and ignore the sensation! The actual bathroom was a huge affair with a stone floor. There was a small raised platform at one end, which acted as a stool, so to speak. It was on this that one was supposed to sit and scrub oneself squeaky clean. But with all the interesting sounds coming in through the low windows, the intention was to just rush through the bath and go outside in the cool, scented yard! The bath water was also heated in a brass gas-lit heater, like a geyser running on fire instead of electricity. But most days, despite the low temperatures, instead of taking a sensible, prosaic hot water bath, we went swimming with the fishes!

The gin had huge machines for sorting the cotton and making bales, and the entire process needed a decent amount of water. To acquire this, a big, deep well had been dug up on the premises, and a pool was also built.

This is where we were taught how to swim. And it was all in a very traditional way; the floater used to teach us was a sealed tin of vegetable ghee that was tied on our backs. This worked very well and kept me afloat during all my pathetic attempts to do a dog paddle, a breast stroke or just plain freestyle. Initially, we swam in the tank, and as we progressed a bit, we were made to swim in the big, deep well.

To access the water, which was a good twenty-five plus feet below, we had to climb down a scary ladder fixed to the side of the well, and though one of my young uncles was brave enough to dive from the very top of the well, none of us ever dared to do that! The water was very cold as the source was an underground spring. It was filled with small fish and a few turtles who splashed off the edge where they would be trying to sun themselves when we entered the water. One hears of the exclusive spas where your feet are cleaned by the fish nibbling the dead skin off your heels; well, here, our entire body was exfoliated thanks to the over-attentive members of the Pisces group. Some of them were too enthusiastic and would give painful nips and, occasionally, draw blood.

Despite this, our forays into the well continued, for the experience was totally unique: any sound made in the well (there were plenty of gasps and snorts as we newbies took in more water than air) echoed and reverberated as if in a cathedral; and instead of making us feel claustrophobic, the high walls seemed to make us feel closer in a familial way. The fish, turtles and the occasional bird nesting on the side seemed to constitute a mini-world to us for the hour that we swam. Upon getting out, Bappa made us take a big tablespoon of 'Doctor's brandy' and boy, oh boy! It was that disgusting! But it was not bad enough to keep us from swimming the next day because that was the condition set by Bappa in the hopes of preventing colds and coughs—and it generally worked, too!

Another beloved memory I have of the cotton gin is walking down a broad lane lined by huge cork trees in full bloom, scenting the entire surroundings with their lovely fragrance. The trees stood tall and proud, and the flowers hung down in sweet-smelling bunches. The whole lane would be covered in a layer of flowers that dropped down to the ground with the slightest gust of wind. Us cousins would gather all the fresh ones in bunches and create tattered flower arrangements. My aunt would weave them into garlands using just their long stalks. In those days, we girls had long hair, and these garlands would be pinned onto our braids. Now, that's a perfume for you—fragrant, natural and for free!

Just beyond the cork trees would be huge mountains of cotton, kept under tin roofs waiting to be deseeded. These soft white mountains were our playground! Much to the disgust of all the workers, we would climb up over bales onto the top of the fluffy, snowy-white mountain, and the thrill we got was no less than having scaled Mount Everest! At that point in our lives, we had never ever seen real snow, but we pretended that these mounds were indeed made of snow and created igloos and snowmen, all of which were speckled with the black seeds of cotton. We would burrow into the cotton or fling ourselves onto big piles and emerge with wisps sticking to us, making us look like we'd run away from a lunatic asylum. The hysterical laughter did nothing to dissuade the impression! But the cotton was rather itchy, and after some time, we had to come away and dust ourselves down thoroughly. But stray wisps clung persistently to the clothing, and so we continued scratching ourselves all over like a troop of monkeys!

This trip to our hometown was extremely educational for me where fauna was concerned because the countryside was still mainly unspoilt; the farms still looked like farms rather than chequered plots of land divided by a ruler; the meandering village lanes were still dust tracks on which you often met a bullock powered cart, and people were still friendly and welcoming, with no signs of "Trespassers will be prosecuted" hung on gates! They did not mind a bunch of greenhorns wandering around on their land oohing and aahing over stuff—if anything, they were highly amused! We would get up early in the morning, have breakfast and be off exploring, giving heed to the call of these inviting tracks.

Smokey, the dog and faithful companion, would often run on ahead with his tongue hanging out, giving warning barks to any errant farm dog who dared glance at us. On both sides would be green living fences of some sort of cacti, thorny bushes or even colourful thick hedges of Lantana. There would be an occasional break in this fence where a tall neem tree or a drumstick tree would sprout. Occasionally, the whole lane would look like a green tunnel as the trees on both sides of the track met at the top like soldiers crossing their swords over the heads of VIPs!

It is in these lanes that tai pointed out the trapdoor spider. These are really ingenious architects! The whole trap consists of a small tunnel that is covered in a soft, misty web. The trapdoor at the front end has a hinge also made from cobweb. Generally, a spider would wait inside the burrow, holding the door shut with its front legs from inside. Along comes a poor unsuspecting ant or grasshopper poking around for food and mistakenly walks over some of the web threads. Wham! The spider drops the trapdoor, grabs the poor victim and drags it into its burrow! All over in a few milliseconds! The cart track had innumerable such shroud-covered webs looking like bits of broken clouds all along the grassy edges.

On the dusty track itself, very often, you could see funnel-shaped depressions—some barely a few millimetres wide and others almost half an inch in diameter. These were also traps but made by the antlion larvae! The funnel walls were smooth and crumbly because of the dry soil. Right at the bottom, unseen below a layer of soil, would be the powerful jaws of the larvae, just waiting to clamp onto some poor ant or beetle who happened to fall into the burrow while foraging for food. The crumbling slope made it impossible for the insect to climb out of the funnel, and its struggle to do so just served as an indicator to the larva who would pop out, grab the victim and drag it down into the sand, and that was the end! These little larvae have hooks at the end of their abdomen, which help them hold on to the soil at the other end so they can't be dragged out of the tunnel by their prey. An effective way of hunting, and yet I find it a bit ruthless as the victim isn't given a sporting chance to escape!

We would continue our ramblings, sometimes peering into the thickets to look at some interesting beetle and sometimes craning our necks to see some bird who would be chattering at us from amongst the branches overhead. Occasionally, we would all burst out into song in different pitches accompanied by the tuneless whistling of my cousin, who had just learnt how to; all in all, setting the right mood for a pleasant expedition.

Soon, our rumbling tummies would warn us of the approaching lunchtime, and we would turn back and let Smokey lead us back home, where a hot lunch awaited. After a good wash, we children, along with my Grandpa, dad and three uncles, would all sit down cross-legged on the floor to eat, regaled by Bappa with daring anecdotes about his childhood and youth—some true, some cleverly embroidered. Somehow, the food ALWAYS tasted better than other times!

The afternoon was siesta time, but puhleeeease—not for us kids! We wouldn't dream of wasting a lovely afternoon sleeping! Sadly, our schools were under the misapprehension that students would forget the content material of their text or even forget how to hold the pencils in a matter of two weeks. So, we all had tons of holiday homework which we had to get out of the way! While the adults rested, we kids grudgingly did an hour of homework daily.

On some days, after the afternoon tea, we would pile into the car and drive down to a nearby reservoir that had a bit of a garden around it. The entrance was guarded by huge banyan trees from which the aerial roots would hang like ropes—a perfect opportunity to try out our Tarzan imitations! Once we had had our fill of the swinging and yodelling, we would proceed through the gates, where there was a vast expanse of scratchy lawn interspersed with some trees. A path would lead us up the side of an embankment, and we could gaze down at the shimmering water of the reservoir.

On calm days, it looked as if a piece of the sky had broken off and fallen to the ground, so beautifully were the clouds reflected! Here, we would unpack the goodies we had brought along and have a glorious picnic! Good food, great scenery with jokes and laughter wafting and mingling with the scent of grass and flowers—a perfect recipe for a day out! On one such day, we spotted a huge bird on the far side of the lake. That was the first owl I had ever seen! It was probably an Eagle owl, which is seen in the area. It is diurnal, and so actively hunts during the day. We couldn't stop talking about it for days, and the size of the owl and its piercing, big eyes increased each time!

The drive back home consisted of a stop at a snake farm. There was a huge pit with loads of venomous snakes slithering around frantically. These were milked for their venom for creating anti-venom. Though used to the sight of snakes, to see so many together was truly mind-boggling. After we had our fill of gawking at these serpents and enough snake stories had been swapped with the keepers, we would pile into our long-suffering car to head home. It would take us up over the last climbs and dips, occasionally squeezing into roadside hedges along the way to make way for bullock carts piled high with cotton heading to the market to be auctioned. These bulls were big animals in a variety of colours with huge, pointed horns adorning their heads. They generally had

Family Festivities

bells around their necks and made a calming, clanging sound as they pulled their load, shaking their heads to try and adjust the yoke which lay heavy on their necks. Finally, we would reach the gin and be deposited in front of the compound gate, where we would get a rousing welcome from both ends of Smokey, the dog—slobbery licks and tail slaps!

All too soon, the precious holiday period would come to an end, and we had to return to our daily grind, but the memories of the trip would provide the fuel for our spirits while we eagerly awaited the next annual "migration" to the familial stomping ground.

CHAPTER 10
EXPANDING HORIZONS

*I*ndia is a vast country with many beautiful, must-see places, and besides our holidays with the grandparents, we had the opportunity to visit quite a few over the years: some nearby and some further afield. Modes of transport varied; train journeys were taken but not so frequently because of connection issues. They could turn out to be quite time-consuming, and schools did not look too kindly upon students who returned late from holidays—much to our sorrow! Hence, our trusty car was our favourite mode of transport. I am told that we got our first car around the time I was born—a Morris Minor.

Very often, my uncle and aunt from Ahmedabad visited. As I mentioned earlier, their children—Vivek and Himangi—and us three girls formed a team, with Shubhangi being the worldly-wise leader whom we looked up to. And on such visits, generally, an outing would be planned. That five kids and four adults (our family and my uncle's) could fit in the tiny little car tells you that everyone was probably below the required BMI despite the humongous amount of food we seemed to consume or that the vehicle was a Tardis in disguise! But this long-suffering vehicle was our trusty steed and companion on many voyages of discovery.

One trip that stands out in my recollections—or at least some unforgettable aspects of it—was to a nearby mountain called Pavagadh. This mountain has a religious significance, and there is a temple situated right at its top with innumerable steps (or so it seemed!) leading up to it! Nowadays, there is a rope-way, I believe, which makes light work of the effort, but personally, I think that it cuts the fun in half as well!

We drove up to the mountain early one morning and left our car at the base of the mountain where there was a rest house and some stalls selling snacks: the quintessential tea and things required to do a pooja at the temple if one so wished. From this 'base camp,' so to speak, we started our climb. The flight of steps went winding upwards, occasionally getting lost from sight as they went round the mountain to suddenly reappear higher up. These steps were made of locally acquired stone, uneven in places, and some were even missing! They were edged with a crumbling, low wall on the open side in the hopes of preventing falls. It also served as a great perch for birds and lizards.

Our initial enthusiasm was absolutely great, with all of us kids skipping upwards like goats, followed by the grownups lugging the picnic hamper, water supply and the picnic mat. After half an hour or so, the distance between the two sets of climbers was markedly missing, and the tempo had cooled down as the warmth of the sun started heating up the rocks. By now, the lizards who had been sunning themselves in the warmth of the morning sun had prudently found cool spots under boulders. The cawing of crows and the chattering rebukes of the palm squirrels who had objected to the intrusion into their privacy had also died down. It was definitely time for a rest stop!

Fortunately, little lay-bys were judiciously provided at appropriate intervals where people could catch their breaths while pretending to be observing the panorama. And beautiful it was! Flat plains rolled out as far as the eye could see, dotted here and there with minuscule-looking villages. You could see winding roads with a few vehicles meandering along them just to disappear into the haze in the distance. There were fields with waving crops and a sparse forest.

During the cooler months, this forest would appear to be on fire with the Palash (or *Kesuda*, as it is known locally) trees in full bloom. The nectar of these brilliant orange flowers—aptly known as 'Flame of the Forest,'—is a favourite with many birds: sunbirds, parakeets, starlings of all sorts, warblers, leaf birds—the list goes on! The flowers attract insects, and where there are insects, bee-eaters, bulbuls, bats, and a variety of reptiles are not far behind! Langur monkeys (a type of Old World monkey) love the tender flowers. The adult langurs could be seen perched on the branches, long tails dangling, picking off the petals and popping them into their mouth with self-satisfied expressions while the younger and less dominant ones would scrounge about under the tree for fallen tasty bits and buds. Some cheeky infants would take advantage of so many dangling tails and would embark on a game of 'I can swing the farthest' using them as vines. Most adult langurs put up with such shenanigans as they were too busy stuffing their mouths. The Palash tree is also a favoured nesting and roosting place for a lot of birds. All in all, you could call it Nature's rest stop for wildlife in general!

Getting back to our rest stop …. This particular spot was a wide ledge with a shallow slope leading down to a couple of ruined structures, probably some older temples or their outbuildings, now in disrepair and abandoned. Some trees had taken root in one of the walls. While the grownups were setting up the picnic, we kids decided to check out the ruins. There was a series of steps leading down through a doorway. I decided this merited further investigation! They led down into a sort of open hallway with a wide opening, looking out onto the rambling hillside. There were some tree roots creeping down the deteriorating stucco walls, which were painted a pale yellow. All was well until one of the tree roots started making its way up the wall! I reacted instinctively and shrieked, and the speed with which I cleared the stairs would have put any Olympic sprinter to shame! My father and uncle rushed to check out the problem. Turns out that I had probably disturbed a snoozing cobra. He/she probably got a bit miffed with all the ruckus and decided to slither away to more peaceful pastures and soon disappeared into the concealing cracks. We sagaciously decided to shift our picnic a few feet away and kept a wary eye on the surroundings the entire time.

After this adrenaline-pumping experience, the rest of the climb seemed to pale in significance and concluded in a very sedate manner, with a sweaty and tired bunch getting into the car and starting on our way back home. My cousin and I were riding shotgun on my uncle's knee (those were the days of sedate speeds and no seat belts!). We had reached the outskirts of the city, when we saw a truly hilarious spectacle: there was a car tyre rolling along the road right in front of us with no one in sight! We all had a hearty laugh, commiserating the poor people who had lost it. All of us came forth with far-fetched theories regarding its origins when, suddenly, my dad realised it was one of ours! Commotion ensued!

He guided the car very, very slowly to the side of the road while everyone held their breath. We fully expected to topple to one side, sparks flying like a scene from the Herbie movies, but we made it without incident. All of us hopped out; Dad took out the spare wheel while my uncle gave chase to the runaway tyre. It so happened that one of the front wheels had managed to come loose and slid off, probably from the rocky road we had traversed in the mountainous area. The momentum of the car had made it continue rolling ahead—a fine example of Newton's First Law of Motion! Soon, both wheels were secured in place, and the rest of the journey was filled with shaky laughter laced with relief because we knew it might not have ended so well. Oh, well! Fortune favours the bold!

Then there was the time my parents took us three sisters to Kerala—'God's own country'—as the state government likes to call it, and God has indeed looked down kindly upon it! Situated along the south-western Malabar coast of the Indian peninsula, it is blessed with beautiful beaches and a luxuriant, undulating rain forest nestled amongst the hills, brimming with wildlife ranging from big mammals like elephants, Indian bison (gaur) and tigers to the Indian giant squirrel, snakes, and a huge variety of insects. There is also a brackish water canal system parallel to the coast, known as the backwaters. A thriving tourist trade operates houseboats for hire on these water channels: from ultra-luxurious, mini floating palaces to rustic, basic ones; it all depends on how much your purse can stretch. Kerala is also very rich culturally, with a lot of beautiful old buildings, including palaces, temples, churches and mosques.

As you can guess, there was plenty to see and do—a trip of many new experiences, including an extremely momentous one because this was the very first time we kids ever sat in an aeroplane! I remember it was an Avro aircraft, a tiny twenty-five or thirty-seater. I was all agog to be flying like a bird and could barely keep still in the tiny Air Force run airport that had just a couple of domestic flights daily. Finally, it was boarding time! We walked across the tarmac to where the aircraft seemed to be grumbling away with its huge propellers rotating slowly as last-minute checks were being done. We climbed up the short ladder and entered the aircraft. I looked around wide-eyed, expecting something out of this world, but was brought down to earth rudely. I blurted out loudly, "This looks exactly like a bus!" My dad shushed me and herded me to my seat while other people gave us amused glances. We were shown how to strap on the seatbelt, the aircraft doors were shut, and the gentle rumble turned into an ear-shattering roar as we taxied towards the runway. After a bone-shaking dash down the airstrip, we finally took off into the wide blue yonder!

After a connecting flight from Bombay (as Mumbai was known then), we reached our final airport of

Trivandrum (current Thiruvananthapuram). Dad had planned the trip along with a friend who was originally from Kerala. We were received by some relatives of this person at the airport and whisked off in a car to their home, where we had the most delicious meal consisting of coconut-based stews, fried fish and *payasam* (a sweet dish). We were fascinated by their home, which looked quite different from ours, mainly because they had traditional decor with huge brass lamps and traditional bright-coloured prints on the soft furnishings. Being a rainforest climate, the plants in the garden seemed to be right out of a magazine with big, lush leaves and vibrant coloured flowers. And, of course, the traditional hospitality left us wanting for nothing. All in all, a wonderful experience!

The next couple of days were spent exploring the city, its beautiful museums filled with gorgeous paintings by Raja Ravi Varma, the renowned Indian painter. From there, we went to the town of Chaganacherry, where we had been put up at a guesthouse. I have memories of the rain-lashed yard, overrun with weeds, having a few enormous jack trees from which suspended the pendulous fruit like big green, armoured balloons! Their stalks looked too flimsy for such a heavy load, but the fruits hung on grimly to the tree trunks, easily withstanding the stormy weather.

The actual accommodation was a dated building with a low, covered veranda in the front onto which the individual rooms opened out. My parents got one room, and we sisters had a separate one! That made us feel all grown up and responsible! We were exploring our territory, so to speak, and my sister decided that the washroom needed to be inaugurated as well! I heard the door close as she disappeared into its gloomy depths. I was busy choosing my bed and exploring the room. But the next moment, the bathroom door was pulled open, and my panic-stricken sister shot out like a bullet from the bathroom! She stuttered with an ashen face, "T...t... there is a snake in the bathroom!" We rushed over and informed the grownups, and there was an immediate stampede to investigate. Feeling brave because of the adult presence, we also followed. There was a slatted glass window above the toilet with a fine wire mesh on it. A snake had made its way up the outside wall and squeezed itself into the space between the mesh and the slats. The poor thing's burrow had probably been flooded, and it just wanted a nice dry place to shelter, I guess. Unfortunately, it had to be evicted so that we could use the facilities without having to glance over the shoulder constantly! After this experience, we were very assiduous in all our room checks. We were used to the sight of snakes in our yard, but the idea of sharing a living space with them was nerve-racking!

On this trip, besides the aeroplane trip, there were many first experiences for me: I saw my first raw cashew fruit; it was the first time I saw pepper growing on a tree (and not in a bottle, imagine that!); I was shown my very first civet cat (unfortunately caught by a farmer to be released elsewhere as they are considered pests) and the first elephants in the wild! Now, that was a real treat!

This truly amazing experience was at the Periyar National Park, named after the Periyar River, which flows through it. A dam has been built across this river, resulting in the formation of a huge reservoir. This man-made lake attracts all species of life—for water and for the plentiful fish in the lake. We travelled by car from our guesthouse to the sanctuary. The journey itself was truly heart-warming for nature lovers; the long, narrow road went through what seemed like a continuous series of villages with houses having sloping roofs (a must because Kerala receives very heavy rainfall) and green gardens with colourful flowers. The ever-present coconut trees lined the roads like tall soldiers standing guard. They seemed to whisper to each other continuously as their long, tattered leaves rustled in the breeze. Then, the road started winding through mountainous terrain. The vegetation changed to a dense green forest that seemed to be slumbering in the early morn, sleepily tucked up in the fluffy, low clouds that wrapped themselves lovingly around the tall, evergreen trees. We finally reached the town of Thekkady from where we were to enter the Periyar National Park.

A choice of a jeep safari or water safari is offered by the authorities. Both are equally fascinating! I remember the boats manoeuvring through the submerged trees sticking out of the water while herds of spotted deer grazed on the far edge of the lake. There were a lot of aquatic birds as well: cormorants sat with their wings akimbo, drying off their wings for the next dive, kingfishers perched on branches keeping a sharp look-out for unsuspecting fish, pond herons crouched on the water's edge like a mugger hiding in the shadows waiting for a victim and the cattle egrets skulked around the heels of the deer or the odd gaur in the hopes of catching the bugs which were disturbed by the hooves of the grazing animals. We were soon graced by the presence of an entire elephant herd: from the ponderous matriarch strolling ahead and on the lookout for hidden danger down to cute, gambolling babies who kept getting in the way of their mothers and aunts. A lot of them entered the water, and it was a treat to watch them sucking up gallons of water in their trunks and spraying it on their backs, visibly enjoying the cooling spray. Elephants are so lucky—they have a built-in shower!

The dense forest was filled with calls of a variety of birds. Palm squirrels skittered across the leaf-strewn forest floor. A curious mongoose sat up to observe us and, deciding that we did not look too threatening, scurried across the path. High up in the trees, one could see the flamboyant rust-coloured Malabar squirrels dashing from branch to branch, chasing each other like bolts of red-brown lightning with the occasional cream-coloured flash when they flicked their tails. Grey hornbills swooped around, looking for wild figs. We did hear peacocks sound the alarm for a tiger, but unfortunately for us, we did not catch a glimpse of the big cat. An occasional monkey call would reverberate through the peaceful scene and would promptly be answered by another one till the air was filled with sounds of a monkey Philharmonic symphony equivalent ... rising to a crescendo and slowly dying down. A truly memorable experience and a very satisfying trip, indeed!

One of my dad's colleagues was quite impressed by all the travelling we managed to do by car. He expressed a wish to join us on one such journey in his own car with his family—two kids around our ages and the lady of the house, of course! And so, a trip to the nearby Saurashtra region (in the state of Gujarat) was planned. The routes were plotted on a series of maps. My dad had a lot of these road maps which had been folded and unfolded so often that they were falling apart. They were lovingly and carefully stuck with Cellotape and were part of our essential gear in those days when no Google Maps existed. Various routes were marked out on them with different colours, important notes were mentioned on the sides, and rest stops were marked; if they could have talked, those maps would have told a great many enthralling tales indeed!

So, the routes were meticulously plotted, bags and picnic hampers were packed, and we set forth one fine morning in two cars. There were quite a few beautiful places on the itinerary; one of the most memorable spots was the beautiful beach of Chorwad in the Junagadh district. We stayed at a lovely palace-turned-hotel just on the beach. This meant that most of our free time was spent on the beach. There were a great many activities to do here: watching the fisher folk bring in the day's fresh catch early in the morning, exploring rock pools for the marine life which got trapped in them at ebb tide, building the stereotypical sand castles with turrets plus a moat and of course splashing about at the water's edge.

The beach in these parts is basically very rocky, with massive boulders sticking out of the water. There are also strong currents throwing up huge waves which lash the rocks with great force; not exactly conducive to a gentle dog paddle, but still, there is something very thrilling and elemental about the feel of the spray in your face and the roar of the massive waves as they dashed up the beach as if trying to grab you by the ankles!

One evening, we found a huge flat boulder like a raised platform on the beach. The waves rolled in, looking deceptively gentle and were quite a good way away. So, we decided to have a sort of picnic on the rocks. It was a lot of fun! We all sang ourselves hoarse, and we kids had a gala time dancing around, putting up an impromptu show while the grown-ups kept up a beat by clapping. We were all enjoying ourselves so much that we did not realise when darkness fell. When we saw the hotel lights come on, the adults declared time up, and we started clambering down the rocks to walk back—but the beach had disappeared! Instead, there were menacing waves lurking around the base of the rocks! We had been having so much fun that we had not realised the tide had crept in! The rocks would be submerged in a matter of a few minutes. Panic ensued! We switched on a couple of torches to try and find a safe path over the slippery rocks. The typical Indian modesty went for a ride, and my mom and the other lady hitched up their sarees, or shall I say, they "rose" to the occasion! Each lady held on to their youngest and skipped from one rock to another towards safety. Fortunately for us, except for a few slips and grazes, we managed to reach dry sand in one piece. The adage 'time flies by when you are having fun' was brought home to us quite succinctly!

Junagadh town has a rich history. It has ancient forts, temples, mosques and of course, modern-day places to visit are the museums which guide you through the colourful history. The area is rather famous for its handmade and brilliantly coloured cloth. This region is quite arid, so traditional clothes have vivid hues to brighten up the mood and can be spotted from afar easily in the bland background. The traditional clothes also have a lot of sequins, so the local ladies seem to sparkle and shimmer as they walk, as if hundreds of fireflies were sitting on their apparel. *Bandhani* sarees (tie and dye sarees), sequined handmade cloth puppets and toys are also a speciality. Bedspreads, footwear, wall hangings—you name it, they make it—all with the ever-present sequins!

Along with the usual touristy stuff, we decided to see the local zoo as well. I guess a zoo is always on the agenda when there are kids. It was a regular sort of zoo, with the usual crocodiles, a variety of birds, tigers and lions. Now, we are an animal-crazy family—you couldn't help but notice it by now! We tend to feel that animals have rights, too! We were trying to be respectful to the confined animals and were observing them quietly as they went about their usual activities in their cages. My dad and his colleague took a few photos of them and us kids in the same frame; we were obviously considered to be kindred spirits! Most of the animals were curious and came pretty near the cage bars to check out the camera. The lion, however, was pretty camera-shy! After all, he was one of the zoo's main attractions and probably had enough of the paparazzi trying to get his pictures! He sat facing the wall and sulking. We hung around for a bit, and then my dad decided there wasn't much point in waiting for his majesty to get into the right pose; there were other cages to view. But the other gentleman just HAD to have a picture! He waved his arms around and did a mad little jig trying to get the lion to look at the camera, making weird sounds which, I guess, he fancied sounded like a lion love song. After about five minutes of his inspired efforts, there was a reaction from the king of the jungle; he stirred from his corner, looked around at the cavorting human and walked over to him. The "uncle," as we respectfully call all older males in India, got his camera into position, waiting for the perfect shot, when the lion coolly turned around and sprayed the poor man very accurately and intentionally with his own personal brand of 'perfume'! Uncle was flabbergasted and dripping—well and truly marked as lion property! For a few seconds, we were just too shocked to react! Then, the penny fell, and most of us just fell down giggling hysterically while the adults covered up smirks and tried to find ways of getting the target cleaned up! It was soon borne upon us that a big cat urine smell is not something which comes off easily from clothes or car seats! Now, that was one trip we weren't likely to forget in a hurry.

This particular lion was a 'home-grown' one, so to speak. This is the only area in the entire world where you can find the Asiatic lion in the wild. In the olden days, the rulers of Junagadh had created their personal hunting grounds near the town where they would entertain the royal guests by organising hunting trips. Thanks to the over-enthusiasm of some gun-toting men who thought that killing the disadvantaged wildlife was macho, the lions were almost totally wiped out till, at the end of the 19th century, the then Nawab was urged to protect the last few remaining lions. Finally, in 1965, the area was declared as the Sasan Gir Wildlife Sanctuary.

Being in the area, this national park was naturally high on our to-visit list. The exact route and stay are a bit of a blur as it feels like it was aeons ago, but the safari itself was thrilling as it was the first big cat safari I ever took. The forest was a dry, deciduous type with stretches of grassland. We were loaded into a safari jeep near the entrance of the park, and then we hurtled along a dusty, uneven track to where the rangers had spotted the lions. It was a hot day, and a whole pride was stretched out, panting in the shade of some acacia trees. All the jeeps lined up pretty close to them, and I half expected some of the big, mangy-maned males to jump into the jeep with us! In fact, a couple of them did raise their heads as our vehicles edged nearer, and then they decided it was too much of an effort and promptly flopped back onto the dusty ground. I had half expected to be chased down by roaring, bloodthirsty beasts, running madly and escaping by the skin of our teeth—a bit akin to some cheap movie scene.

Despite the anti-climax (and a distinct sense of relief), it was extremely thrilling to see the powerful animals in their own natural setting. We also observed wild boar in the vicinity and the ever-present spotted deer—the staple diet of the lions. But they sensed that the lions were not really in hunting mode, so all was relatively peaceful except for the chattering langur (a type of monkey, as I have mentioned earlier), which shouted rude somethings to the big cats and warned other animals of their presence. As we were traversing another path in search of other resident wild animals, very unexpectedly, a big lioness emerged from some bushes and coolly crossed the path right in front of us with nary a glance in our direction! Obviously, we were too lowly to be spared a glance by her majesty—thank goodness for that!

In those days, there was an ongoing tussle between the wildlife department and the local villagers on grazing rights. The officials would have preferred that the cattle be kept out of the forest. Nonetheless, the villagers were adamant as it was traditionally used by the villages for grazing as well as a source of wood for fuel. This, of course, meant that cattle were attacked by lions which obviously caused a great deal of friction between the lions and the villagers. The forest cover was being reduced because people were chopping down trees illegally, and of course, poaching was a major threat—as an act of retaliation for lost cattle and for the black market. Sadly, there were even cases of poisoning the wildlife. One can understand the concern the villagers had; it was a matter of safety and livelihood. Sadly, human beings have taken over the homes of a lot of wild animals. Unlike people, these poor things are unable to hold demonstrations or go on strikes to bring their plight to notice. They either struggle to survive alongside humans or perish while trying.

But these problems have been vastly reduced by showing the local population the advantages of having a world-famous national park at their doorstep; livelihood has increased as the forest department acts as a major employer for the surrounding villages, and tourism has brought in a lot of side business, again helping the local communities to thrive. The government also took a lot of measures to teach the villagers how to cohabit with the wild animals. They are encouraged to look upon the lions as a source of pride and to act as their guardians. The attitudes have changed considerably. Being compensated to an extent for any errant attack on the cattle has also helped soften attitudes. Long live the king of the jungle!

CHAPTER 11

MIGRATING NORTHWARD

*N*orthern India is as beautiful and bountiful as southern India, but in a different way. This is because of the geographical differences, of course. Part of the majestic Himalayan range forms a natural border between India and some of its northern neighbours. A lot of the major Indian rivers find their origin in the glaciers of these towering mountains. Nestled amongst the mountains are a number of hill stations which are popular as honeymoon destinations and family getaways, especially in the summers. One such place we visited as a family was Nainital, a town located in the Kumaon section of the Indian Himalayas (the very same Kumaon featured in the famous book by Jim Corbett called *The Man-Eaters of Kumaon*. The name "Naini-tal" literally means nine lakes. Thus, this area is also known as the

Lake District. My two cousins from Ahmedabad—Vivek and Himangi—accompanied us on this trip.

We caught a flight to Delhi, and from there, we got on a bus which took us up the winding roads through the mountains to our goal. The scenery along the way was absolutely breathtaking! Some sections of the route passed through forested areas with tall coniferous trees and dense undergrowth, and then, we would suddenly come up on a fast-flowing rivulet with froth-flecked wavelets tumbling madly over boulders, throwing up spray on the moss-covered rocks by its side. Occasionally, you could spot a heron or an egret trying to catch their lunch in the swiftly flowing cold waters.

The bus wheezed its way slowly up the curves, the exhaust giving out nauseous fumes from an overworked engine. Himangi tends to get car sick, so we had packed quite a few plastic bags, which proved handy. Though she was just a young kid—about eight years old—she was very stoic about the whole affair and quietly went about the process of emptying her stomach contents into plastic bags without bothering anyone! The monotonous droning of the engine acted as a potent lullaby, with the slow and steady rocking motion of the bus acting like a huge metallic cradle. Many people nodded off, including Shubhangi tai and Vivek. Both of them love a good nap and fall asleep at the drop of a hat. The sharp curves of the road meant that the sleepy "heads" in the bus lolled from one side to the other as the bus turned direction.

Tai, Vivek and I sat in one seat with the others behind us, with me at the window seat, Vivek in the middle and tai at the far end, which had a convenient pole for holding on to. The seat in front of us was occupied by a young couple very evidently on their honeymoon. They had simpered, giggled and stuck close to each other from the very beginning of the journey, as honeymooners are wont to do. Being typical kids, we thought the whole scene was simply yucky! The groom was in the same category as my sister and cousin and could not resist the sandman; he, too, soon fell asleep and joined the head lolling bus community. With each curve of the road, Vivek's head would rest either on my shoulder or tai's, depending upon the direction, while tai had the bus pole to rest her head on, and so was relatively secure. Occasionally, the bus would lurch over uneven surfaces, causing the napping heads to rock back and forth. When we came across a particularly bumpy stretch, my father told me to support Vivek's nodding head—and just in time, too! The bus went over a big pothole, which caused a mini 'bus-quake,' and all the sleeping beauties were almost thrown from their seats. I had been holding Vivek by the shoulder so he was not affected too much. Shubhangi tai had been holding on to the pole while dozing, so she was also alright, but the poor newly married gent in front of us did not have such luck; his bride had been looking out of the window at the time with nary a care for her napping spouse! He jerked forward sharply and banged his head with a loud thud on the metal bar of the seat in front of him! Now, that was truly a rude awakening! The image of the poor, dazed chap looking around him while rubbing the swiftly rising bump on his forehead will remain etched in my mind forever! What a start to a honeymoon!

After a long and tiring journey, we finally reached our destination and got off with our luggage, which was bulky thanks to all the woollies. We looked around for a cab to transport us to our company guest house, but none seemed available. After a long wait, we hired a couple of cycle rickshaws, dumped our luggage in them and trundled slowly all the way to our hotel. It was located on a steep hillside which seemed insurmountable after the long day, but there was more to come! Once inside, we realised our accommodation was on the third floor, and the only way to reach it was to climb up three flights of very narrow, wooden stairs! The day seemed never-ending!

The next morning, we realised that summer in Nainital was WAY colder than winter in Gujarat! The water in the taps was absolutely freezing! The routine tasks of brushing teeth and washing hands were sheer torture! The bath water was very nice and hot, but unfortunately, baths had to end, and we had to return to freezing rooms.

The only form of heating was from a room heater, which glowed red all the while we were in the room.

All this cold weather led to healthy appetites. We would be served food in our apartment. Meals consisted of steaming chole-bhature (chickpea curry with pooris) or piping hot parathas with equally hot curries. The kitchen was on the ground floor. With five starving kids and two equally hungry adults, the amount of food which had to be ferried up was immense and entailed innumerable trips up and down the stairs for our attendant. I am sure that by the time we left, we had put on quite a bit of weight, whereas he had lost a lot!

Every morning, after a hearty breakfast, we would head down to the main lake for a vigorous session of rowing. This was the first time we had ever handled oars, so we ended up going around in circles, feeling quite dizzy! Finally, after a couple of days, we were all in reasonable coordination, and we could execute a decent ride along the perimeter of the lake. The lake itself is pretty deep. One can't see the bottom, but there were shoals of fish begging tourists for food, mouths opening and closing in expectation; there were also a lot of honking geese who were not so polite and would advance aggressively towards you, demanding grub. Once we finished our boating, we would sneak past these avian haranguers and dash to our guest house for a bath and breakfast. The rest of the day was given over to exploring surrounding areas and generally being the typical tourists. One morning, though, we got up very early and trudged in almost complete darkness to a point very aptly called the "Sunrise Point," from whence you can see the lofty Trishul peak. Though we kids cribbed a lot about having to get out of our warm beds at such an ungodly hour, I must admit the view was fantastic! As the sun struggled to climb up over the mountains, the range was bathed in a deep red glow which changed to a lighter orange as time passed. When the light finally reached the mountain peaks, the snow-clad slopes reflected the light and glowed like molten lava! The entire section of the Himalayas visible from the viewpoint was outlined in the soft orange glow. We held our breath and watched the heavenly scenario till the sun rose up over the mountains, and the peaks returned to the dazzling white with flecks of craggy brown they were throughout the day—a cookies and cream ice cream appearance!

At night, to give our poor hotel attendant a break, we would eat dinner in some other eatery—generally one of the stalls which served steaming hot chole-bhature in earthen pots—straight off the stove! The time of our visit coincided with the festival of light—Diwali—and the whole town of Nainital was lit up with small lamps edging the buildings. The houses up on the dark slopes looked as if a horde of twinkling fireflies had descended upon them—a very picturesque scene indeed! Diwali is also the time for firecrackers, and the streets were full of kids and grownups bursting a ton of them. A most dangerous place to do so, I must say.

There is a flat, round cracker called the *'chakri'*, which is supposed to be placed in a big, deep plate or flat container and then lit. The lit end basically acts like the propellant of a rocket, creating a thrust which propels the flat cracker. Being in a container controls the direction. Unfortunately, the crowd in the street seemed to lack plates, and they lit these *chakris* right on the street. Soon, the street was being crisscrossed by flaming little wheels whizzing in random directions. I am not ashamed to admit that I am wary of crackers, and fate decided to reinforce my concern. One of the swirling *chakris* suddenly changed directions and slipped under the long gown I happened to be wearing. I displayed a nimbleness any mountain goat would have envied and jumped about a couple of feet in the air; fortunately, I managed to make good my escape, but I can tell you that I have never particularly cared for this cracker after this incident.

After dinner, we would stroll through the streets (with me keeping a sharp look-out for errant crackers!) exploring stalls selling local goods, breathing in lungfuls of cold air laden with the delicious scent which was a heady mix of the lemony-woody, pine tree scent wafting down from the slopes and the mouth-watering aroma of the frying bhaturas. We would often end up sitting all in a row on a low wall which edged a steep valley. In the thick darkness cloaking the verdant mountain slopes, you could just make out a few glowing lights of a tiny hamlet in the valley. Occasionally, temple bells would ring out resonantly, and the faint sound of chanting would be carried up to us in the chilly air. The stars twinkled brightly in the unpolluted sky, lending a magical touch to the scenario while we just sat quietly and absorbed it in; as William Wordsworth put it, "What is this life if, full of care, we have no time to stand and stare."

On our return trip back home, which was again via Delhi, we dropped in on some relatives. Lovely folks who had an even lovelier dog called Bhairav! He probably wouldn't have won any prizes in a dog beauty contest as he had the face and body of an Alsatian but the height of a poodle or corgi. Nevertheless, he was a very friendly dog, good-looking with twinkling eyes and an endearing bark. He was also a very intelligent dog. His party trick was counting. The owners would call out a random number between one and ten, and Bhairav would wuff out the exact number of barks. Simply amazing! We were all thoroughly impressed and rewarded each of his efforts with claps and treats. He made a mistake only once in all the times he was asked to show his prowess; he was asked to count to seven, but he barked only six times. After taking a quick glance around at our expectant faces, he quickly added another bark and then sat back, smiling in a self-satisfied manner as we all burst out laughing.

He had been clever enough to guess that he had made a mistake AND then acted upon that thought! The quick-wittedness he showed in his thought process was more admirable than his counting abilities. If I was asked to say something a certain number of times without counting on my finger, it is highly likely that I would commit an error BUT wouldn't be able to pick up on the fact!

On the day of the departure, we piled into a cab and headed to the airport early in the morning. The flight back home was a direct flight from Delhi. We were a pretty big group for a family—five kids and two adults. I am sure in those days when family planning was being fervently promoted, my parents must have received some scathing looks! Mind you, we were quite a well-behaved bunch, if I may say so myself. (I don't think we really bothered the adults except when we were hungry; then, we were like a starving pack of wolves!) At the check-in, the counter staff realised that they did not have seven seats in a row, so we were to be seated in consecutive rows at the tail end of the aircraft. Vinita and Himangi were in the very last row near the flight attendant's station. The flight took off smoothly, and the loud drone cut out the possibility of chatting across the rows. So, we all busied ourselves with the complimentary kid magazines and puzzles.

Our section had a pretty young air hostess who kept glancing sympathetically at the two young girls seated all alone right at the back. They both got extra toffees, which

I felt was rather unfair! Bigger children need more energy; therefore, they need more toffees! Isn't that logical? But no, we did not get the special attention being bestowed on the kiddy-duo. Himangi's very long plaits were admired, and a conversation struck up between the kindly attendant and the girls. The hostess asked Himangi if her parents were on board. Himangi answered truthfully that they weren't; she conveniently forgot to mention that she was travelling with her uncle and aunt. The kind-hearted attendant assumed they had been heartlessly forced to travel alone in the big wide world and immediately took it upon herself to make their flight as cushy as possible. Their supply of toffees was suitably augmented, soft toys were bestowed, and both were plied with juices. I can tell you that the rest of us kids felt a bit peeved at this! My parents, who were seated further up the aircraft, were blissfully oblivious to all this. Unfortunately, the aircraft developed some mysterious technical snag, and our flight was diverted to the nearest airport in Jaipur, Rajasthan—quite a thrill for us, though I am sure my parents did not agree! But when life throws lemons at you, the only thing to do is make lemonade, as they say.

When we landed at Jaipur airport and disembarked, the flight attendants realised that we had two grownups in our entourage and looked a bit taken aback! We all bade them goodbye and, thanked them politely and made our way out. We were informed by the airline that repairs would take a considerable amount of time, so a big coach had been arranged to take all the passengers to a hotel for lunch.

And what a hotel! We were taken to the Rambagh Palace, which was used in the olden days as a royal guesthouse, and later, the Maharaja and his queen took up residence in it. It is a majestic building with long, beautifully polished verandas, strategically placed sofas and chairs overlooking beautifully manicured gardens. There is the typical Rajasthani architecture with a dash of influence from other styles in certain rooms. Tall support columns line the verandahs which were edged with sandstone balustrades and strategically placed marble lattices. On the roof are the typical domes or cupolas which served as lookouts as well as wind towers—a truly magnificent palace converted into a five-star hotel.

This was another first for us! All the gleaming marble, the plush furnishings and the immaculately dressed attendants gliding around offering pre-dinner drinks were a bit overwhelming for us kids, so we were a rather subdued bunch till lunch was served. It was a typical Indian menu with a number of courses—from chutneys and salads to dals and curries, all accompanied by a wide variety of breads and rice dishes. All followed by scrumptious desserts.

As is the Western style, each place setting had the required knives and forks, but Indian meals are not meant to be eaten delicately at the end of a metal implement; we eat our food with gusto and using all our senses, including touch. The satisfaction one gets from breaking the chapati, dipping it in a hot curry and then eating it can never come from using a fork and knife! This may sound uncouth, but eating by hand is an art! Not everyone can do it elegantly unless it is practised. The dominant hand is the only one used to eat, generally, the right one. We are expected to use only the fingers of that hand to break the chapati or mix the rice, and only the fingers are used to transport the food to the mouth, so to say. Now, there were quite a few tourists among the passengers, including a couple from the UK who were sitting next to Shubhangi tai. They were quite bemused when we got down to the task of eating using our fingers, systematically and efficiently demolishing the lovely food on the dazzling silver plates set in front of us. After watching tai for some time, the British gentleman leaned over to her and asked if he could see her hand. Shubhangi tai was a bit taken aback, but having come across other foreigners in our colony, we were used to their curiosity about Indian ways, so she obligingly held out her hand—palm up—for the couple. The couple were surprised to see that her palm was clean and dry, without a speck of food, and that only the fingers bore evidence of any eating activity. It was then that I realised—eating was an art which we kids were better at than some grown-ups!

After the sumptuous lunch, we were told that there was still some time before our flight could depart. So, we had some time to explore the beautiful hotel and its grounds. Wide expanses of immaculate lawns spread out beyond the long verandas. Here and there were beautiful flower beds, and some stunning peacocks strutted in between them, displaying their vibrant coloured tails. A snake charmer had been organised to entertain everyone (something not common now, thank goodness! He did the typical snake charmer thing: played the *pungi* (a flute-like instrument with a bugle in between) to 'tempt' the cobra out from its round cane basket. The poor, uneasy reptile cannot take its eyes off the swaying snake charmer and follows his moments perfectly. Frankly, there is nothing 'charming' about this cruel imprisonment of the snakes. Unfortunately, we were too young to know any better. There was also a huge Indian rock python that was being used as a photo prop. A lot of the tourists, including Shubhangi tai, had a photo taken with the heavy creature carelessly slung around the shoulders like a shawl. Finally, the poor reptiles were allowed to retreat into their containers, and all of us were escorted back to our bus to be transported back to the airport, and we continued our journey uneventfully.

CHAPTER 12

CONTINUUM

*N*ot all our journeys were over great distances and involved a lot of travelling; in fact, some of the best journeys we undertook were to visit my Vivek and Himangi, the Ahmedabad cousins. This involved a car journey of around a couple of hours only. Come a long weekend, and we would pile into the car and head off down a national highway to spend time together. These trips were truly great fun! The main attraction was, of course, the idea of spending time with kinspeople—always a pleasure because we were similar ages with similar likes and dislikes, but the drive itself was pretty alluring.

In those days, the highway wound itself through villages, fields and rivers. One had to watch out for the lumbering lorries driven haphazardly by overworked and underpaid drivers trying to stick to their schedules. The road in those days was just a single-lane road, so overtaking one of these overfilled, lumbering behemoths was really difficult and required skill! But the fantastic scenery and the birdlife one could spot on these roads made up for these nail-biting experiences. Especially during the winter and rainy seasons, there were loads of migratory birds to spot. In those days, one could be treated to the sight of rows of ibis—both the white as well as the black varieties—grazing in the green fields. Occasionally, a pair of Sarus cranes would raise their beautiful red heads out of the long grass, throw back their heads and let out their loud yet strangely delicate calls as if just to declare their thrill at being alive in a beautiful and bountiful place. Though these birds are not migratory, they do tend to move short distances to fresh, wet areas in search of food—fish, frogs, insects, grains, some plants—a lot of stuff is grist to their mill! Unfortunately, in recent times, their population has declined considerably, thanks to the destruction of habitat and, of course, the ever-present insecticides! These situations apply to other species as well, and nowadays, one no longer gets to see the variety and abundance of birdlife we saw in those days.

Anyway, to get back to happier times, there were also the flamboyant peacocks strutting about showing off their beautiful plumage to their adoring females, who are much plainer in comparison. They would pose on low-hanging branches of acacias, or some of them specifically chose open patches as a stage to spread out their fluorescent feathers and twirl round and round in slow circles so that the females wouldn't miss any inch of their virile bodies!

There were also the cattle egrets running in between the hooves of the grazing cattle, madly stabbing the air in the hopes of catching the insects which were hopping out of the way! The water-logged ditches provided the perfect home for pond herons who sat hunched over the water's edge, glaring at the surface as if willing some fish to fly into their lance-like beaks! As we drove alongside the field edges, a troop of langurs would swing along with us occasionally for some distance, sometimes scaring a waiting kingfisher or a well-concealed hornbill into taking flight. There have been quite a few times when Dad had to slam on the brakes to avoid a mongoose or a snake that decided suddenly that the pastures were greener on the other side of the highway! The jungle babblers would just cock their heads at the ensuing commotion, shrug their already dishevelled grey plumage and gaze disdainfully with a white-eyed, mad-looking gaze cackling harshly.

At times, we would stop at an AMUL Dairy outlet that was right off the road and grab a few cold shakes and chocolates. I love these chocolates even to this day, but somehow, they tasted much better in those surrounds.

Just before entering Ahmedabad city, we had to cross the massive and hugely stinky city dump. But birdlife thrived even here! There were vultures (sadly, though, no more), occasional shikras and scores of circling pariah kites were also part of the feathered community here. A great many birds could be seen flying in seemingly chaotic ways, and you couldn't help but wonder why there were no mid-air collisions! The kites would even perch on the electrical lines that ran alongside the road. You could then really make out their beautiful brown and black markings. If you could bear the stench of the garbage and roll down the car windows, you could hear the racket all the birds made. Finally, we would reach our destination, and a different sort of racket ensued … five exuberant kids can contribute a lot towards noise pollution!

Those were the days! We were all avid fans of old westerns, and occasionally, the neighbours were treated (or mistreated!) to loud music along with enthusiastic vocal accompaniment. We may not have known all the lyrics, but that did not deter us—we would just make up our own! There were also visits to the local municipal library, which was well-stocked indeed. The children's section had the whole range of Tintin and Asterix comic books. At that point of time, they were too expensive for us to buy, so I poured over them for hours in the said library, trying to read as many as possible, until my cousin would get bored and drag me back home. To entertain us, the adults would take us to the movies. I remember the time we went to see *Guns of Navarone*. The theatre was packed, and all we got were the front-row seats. Watching Gregory Peck and the rest of the cast scale the terrifying mountains of the fictional island of Navarone was a magnificent scene as it is, but to watch it from the front seats felt much more realistic—as good as a three-dimensional effect: one could almost feel the spray of the sea and the rain! Then, there was the movie *Hatari*, one of the first movies I saw that was based on animals and ACTUALLY showed animals! Till today, I remember the scene where the rhino is being chased. I also recollect being upset for all the animals who were being harassed by the trappers! The *Baby Elephant Walk* from this movie is still one of my favourite compositions.

One great inspiration for me in those days was Dr. Ruben David, who had been the architect of the Ahmedabad Zoo. He was reputed to be a great reformist, even in those days, where zoos were concerned. The enclosures created were much better and more natural-looking than most other zoos I had seen. He was also reputed to be on a name basis with each animal, and we were told he would have some animal or the other taken out of its enclosure and into his office very often, probably for a tete-a-tete! He is said to have had a great understanding and empathy towards all the animals. After hearing all the amazing stories about Dr. Ruben, I wanted to be just like him—an animal whisperer!

There was also a wider variety of animals in this zoo than in most other Indian zoos. At one time, there was a fascinating species called Binturong or Bearcat. These are very cute-looking mammals with dark and shaggy fur and a long, bushy tail. They are the only Asian mammals with a prehensile tail, which they use to help them climb and anchor themselves to the trees while sleeping. Weird fact: they are supposed to smell like buttered popcorn! We went over to see this star attraction, and the cage was empty! Gullible kids that we were, someone told us—I think it was a zoo janitor—that these animals possess the ability to turn themselves invisible. We fell for the line, hook, line and sinker! For a long time, I believed that binturongs are sort of super animals or beings from other planets who know the invisibility spell. Turns out, these animals are nocturnal and spend the day sleeping high up in branches, and they often spread their huge furry tail over their bodies, effectively camouflaging themselves from prying eyes! This simple explanation took out all the mystique I had attached to a binturong, but the fact remains, I have yet to see a real live binturong in the flesh!

There was generally a return visit by cousins Vivek and Himangi as well during the long summer break. Probably, my mom and aunt had a sort of deal to take care of the children turn by turn so that they both could get a child-free breather! Those days hold some truly sweet memories—and I mean SWEET! Summer is the mango season in India. A wide variety is available: from raw ones to be cut and eaten to some types which are specifically for making pulp, which tastes oh-so-delicious, especially when accompanied by pooris and potato curry! There are some varieties which are used raw for making pickles, jams and also a very delicious cooling drink called *panha*. As you can imagine, all this implied a busy time for my mom! There were raw mangoes to be peeled, chopped, grated, boiled or salted to be kept out in the sun for the relishes.

This was also the time when all of us cousins would go for an early morning swim in the pool located in the petrochemical plant township next to our colony. We would rise and shine bright and early in the morning. As there was no school, we had no objections to getting up early—the earlier we woke up, the more fun could be crammed into the day!

After a glass of milk, we would head off down the road carrying a fresh set of clothes. It was a fifteen-minute walk between rows of houses with pretty gardens, adding to the pleasure of a walk in the still-cool morning. At the pool house, we would rush to take the mandatory pre-swim shower, and then a quick dash and a mad cannonball jump would land us into the cold, chlorine-scented pool! At that hour, the pool was generally empty, and we would have a gala time playing in the shallows. Our favourite game was throwing a big coin in the water and trying to retrieve it. It was not easy at all as the wavelengths made pinpointing the coin location a big challenge; it would wink deceptively in one spot, and the moment you dived under the water, it would have shifted its location! The law of refraction was made abundantly clear to us!

We also liked to compete about who could hold their breath for the longest time. The idea was to start at one end of the breadth of the pool and reach the other. Most of the time, we would erupt from the water about three quarters of the way, gasping for breath—the fun was in trying. My cousins completed their swimming training in this very pool.

After the one hour allowed us, we had to get out of the pool, hit the showers and walk back home, tired and dragging our feet. By now, the hunger pangs would strike. After reaching home, Mum would serve us a MASSIVE plate of sliced mangoes, and we would sit in a circle to eat the delicious fruit for breakfast. Those were the days!

I had quite a load of relatives from my maternal side on whom we would descend occasionally by the carload. One of my maternal uncles lived in a town called Sakharwadi with his wife and two boys. He worked in the big sugar factory located here. How could working in a SUGAR mill constitute a job? That was the thought I had when I came upon this information—I mean, how can being in any place which makes sweet stuff be anything but fun? Sadly, those days of naivety have long gone!

Sakharwadi is situated in the sugarcane-producing district of Satara in the state of Maharashtra. An efficient system of canals has been set up to ease any water woes and thus help the farmers increase the production of sugarcane. These waterways are full of aquatic life. My cousins took us down for a refreshing dunk in a nearby canal. We were a little vary as we were used to chlorinated swimming pools, and swimming in muddy brown waters with waving weeds pulling at our legs was a bit unnerving, so while the local cousins did running jumps with careless glee in the gently flowing water, we city slickers contented ourselves with dangling our legs in the canal. Suddenly, one of the cousins reached down and pulled out a huge crab from the water and stuck it in my face! Having a vividly coloured crab clicking menacing-looking claws like in-built castanets in your face is not a great experience at all! Now that we knew the canal had such gigantic crustaceans in its murky depths, we hastily decided that wading in it was as dangerous as swimming. My cousins carelessly caught a few more crabs and put them in a water-filled jar for observation. Once we had our fill of oohing and aahing over them, they went back into the canal, much to their relief AND ours!

As you must have garnered by now, our trips were slightly chaotic (as is wont where kids are concerned) yet highly enjoyable. If need be, our pets were also taken along for the trip. Occasionally, Robby (our beloved

German shepherd) would accompany us. Unfortunately, he was a huge, hot, hairy and slobbery boy who would take up considerable space in the car, which was rather tough on everyone, including the dog, on hot summer days as our car had no air conditioning. So, such trips were few and far between.

All said and done, all our trips, whether short or long, were thoroughly enjoyable. Thankfully, none of us kids realised that they had educational value as well, else we would have done our best not to let any knowledge sneak into our heads!

It all happened rather NATURALLY!

THE END

POSTFACE

*H*ere ends my attempt at airing any literary skills that may or may not exist in me. There are many more instances which I can remember, but probably they may not be of much interest to anyone else—the sensation of the silky river water slipping through our toes as we waded about trying to get rounded rocks and pebbles for the rocker or the smell of the fresh air as we cycled past the village pond which was dotted with the heads of wallowing buffaloes and edged with foraging cattle egrets and potbellied pigs. Then, there were the fungus gnats and no-see-ums, which seemed to have a penchant for getting into one's ears and fluttered helplessly, trapped in the depths of your ear canal, until you put in some oil and washed them out in a sense. There were also the blue-green caterpillars of the cabbage butterfly, which one could find looping through the home-grown cauliflower—gross for my mom but interesting for me. Even the smell of the damp earth mixed with the aroma of wet leaves was way better than any perfume you could buy off the counter!

Postface

I will leave you here, dear reader, and I do hope that you were entertained enough to be able to drift away from your cares for just a bit; my hope was to make you observe the natural world around us, not just in some rainforest or a mountain range. You can easily find a variety of life forms just in the plot right outside your home or in the parks you go for your picnics or in the sky you look out at through your windows. And I bid you namaste. May you share this world fairly with your fellow creatures, just as Mother Nature intended.

www.ingramcontent.com/pod-product-compliance
Lightning Source LLC
LaVergne TN
LVHW041711070526
838199LV00045B/1297